BREW WARE

How to Find, Adapt & Build Homebrewing Equipment

Karl F. Lutzen and Mark Stevens

Illustrated by Randy Mosher

STOREY

A Storey Publishing Book

Storey Communications, Inc.

The mission of Storey Communications is to serve our customers by publishing practical information that encourages personal independence in harmony with the environment.

Edited by Elizabeth McHale
Cover design by Greg Imhoff
Cover photograph by A. Blake Gardner
Text design by Cynthia McFarland and Meredith Maker
Text production by Susan Bernier and Wanda Harper Joyce
Illustrations by Randy Mosher
Indexed by Northwind Editorial Services

Printed in Canada by WebCom

10 9 8 7 6 5 4 3 2 1

Library of Congress Cataloging-in-Publication Data

Lutzen, Karl F., 1961–
    Brew ware: how to find, adapt, and build homebrewing
equipment/Karl F. Lutzen and Mark Stevens ; illustrated by Randy
Mosher
        p.   cm.
    "A Storey Publishing Book."
    Includes bibliographical references.
    ISBN 0-88266-926-5 (pb : alk. paper)
    1. Brewing—Amateurs' manuals. I. Stevens, Mark, 1960–.

II. Title.
TP570.L88 1996
641.8'73—dc20   96-104
                                                              CIP

ACKNOWLEDGMENTS

We wish to thank our many homebrewing friends who shared ideas with us, shared beers with us, and otherwise encouraged us in this project. We would especially like to acknowledge the help, support, and kind advice of Chris Barnhart, Kinney Baughmann, Jim Busch, Bob Dawson, Kirk Fleming, Keith Hooker, Martin Johnson, Larry Koch, Al Korzonas, Jim Mosser, Jack Mowbray, John Palmer, Roy Price, Ruben Rudd, Jack Schmidling, Gene Thomas and many others, to whom we apologize for overlooking. A special toast to Brewers United for Real Potables (BURP).

And finally, we would like to thank Marc Tewey, brewmaster of Brimstone Brewing Company, of Baltimore, Maryland, for taking the time to explain commercial brewing equipment operation to us and allowing us to photograph his brewery.

CONTENTS

FOREWORD

GETTING INTO THE SPIRIT OF HOMEBREWING

The last decade has seen immense growth in the ranks of homebrewers, just as it has seen immense growth in the number of brewpubs and microbreweries — what has come to be known as the craft brewing industry. In many ways the two feed on each other: The growth of small breweries inspires hobbyists to brew ever-better beer, and the hobby itself serves as a training ground and experimental laboratory for the craft brewing industry. More than a few brewpubs and microbreweries were started by or are staffed by former homebrewers who had the desire and dedication to learn about and brew great beers.

Indeed, much of the spirit of homebrewing is an experimental one. It's the attitude of tinkerers who are unsatisfied with simply brewing good, clean beers. That very attitude leads brewers to experiment with unusual ingredients or unconventional ways of approaching the brewing process. There are some great brewing ideas out there — many of which we undoubtedly have yet to hear about or see in action. The same is true for brewing hardware. In this book, we have tried to give a reasonably comprehensive view of equipment and gadgets used in homebrewing today; however, new gadgets unquestionably will come to market between the time we researched and wrote this book and the time it reaches your bookshelf. And because homebrewers are experimenters and tinkerers, the process will continue. The coming years should see even more great ideas for new equipment and for solving problems as homebrewing continues to grow.

Homebrew supply shops are a vital part of the homebrewing community, providing not only a ready source of ingredients and equipment, but also a ready source of information, tips, and troubleshooting help. The supply shop often serves as a focus point for homebrewers in a local area — a place where homebrewers can meet, form clubs, and find out about homebrewing events, such as competitions or beer festivals. A good, knowledgeable, well-stocked local supplier is a valuable resource.

Our intention in writing *Brew Ware* is to serve the homebrewer and especially the tinkerer — those brewers who are not content with the cheapest or easiest route but who seek out alternatives and ever-better gadgets in their quest for great beer.

So if in *Brew Ware* we show you how to drill a hole in a rubber stopper, it is not because that will be the best approach for everyone, but because that approach best meets the needs of some brewers sometimes. In fact, better solutions (such as the carboy cap) are often available at your local homebrew supply shop, and often at lower cost. Homebrew supply shops can often order the gadgets we describe here, and often at lower cost than you could get by calling the manufacturer directly. But, as we said, our goal in writing this book is to serve the homebrewer, and so we include contact information of the manufacturers so that if you are unable to find a local supplier who carries or is willing to order a gadget that best meets your needs, you can contact the manufacturer to find a supplier who does carry it.

INTRODUCTION

AN OVERVIEW OF BREWING

THE FIVE BASIC STEPS OF BREWING BEER are wort production, boiling, cooling, fermenting, and packaging. Wort production is the creation of a solution of water and the sugars needed for fermentation. For most beginning homebrewers, wort production is simply the blending in a pot of malt extracts and water. For an advanced all-grain brewer, it involves mashing the grains by soaking them in water at an appropriate temperature for an appropriate length of time and then rinsing the grains with water to fully extract the sugars. In the boil, hops are added to the wort and the wort is boiled for at least an hour. The wort is then cooled to a temperature adequate for yeast growth (usually below 80°F). To start fermentation, the mixture is shaken vigorously to aerate it, yeast is added, and the beer is allowed to ferment for several days or weeks. During the fermentation period it may be transferred (or "racked") to another vessel one or more times in an effort to reduce the amount of sediment and improve the beer's clarity. The finished beer is then usually packaged in either bottles or kegs. It's then time for the most important step of all — drinking the finished beer!

A complete examination of all these steps would take a book to explain. Fortunately, that book has already been written. Most basic equipment kits sold at homebrew supply stores today will include a basic introduction to brewing. These instructions will explain, in simple terms, what you need to do to brew better beers, have more control over the finished product, and develop a more complete understanding of brewing ingredients, styles, and processes. If you want a book that fully examines the brewing process in a straightforward, technically sound manner, we recommend *Dave Miller's Homebrewing Guide.*

PREPARING TO BREW

Before you get started, you need to have a recipe in mind (or an ingredient kit with the proper ingredients assembled) and your equipment and work area ready and sanitized. Some brewers like to pre-boil their brewing water or let it sit overnight to drive off the chlorine usually present in municipal water. Pre-warming malt syrups will also help them pour better.

WORT PRODUCTION

For most beginning homebrewers, wort production is easy. You simply pour the malt syrup or powder into a pot of water and stir. For the all-grain brewer, it's an involved process that begins by crushing grain and then adding hot water to reach an appropriate temperature. The target temperature will depend on which type of mashing schedule the brewer is using. The simplest of the mashing schedules is what's known as a single-step infusion mash. For this type of mash, water is added until a temperature in the range of about 148° to about 158°F is reached. This could be preceded by other, lower temperature steps, such as what is called an "acid rest," or perhaps a "protein rest," or both. Each of the different types of steps promote the activity of a different type of enzyme reaction in the grains. After the grains are mashed (i.e., all the starches are converted to sugars), the mash is sparged with water, which is the rinsing of the grains to fully extract the sweet liquid from the grain.

Boiling the Wort

The boil is important for several reasons. It's during the boil that hops are added and their bitterness extracted in a process known as "isomerization." There are also a number of kettle reactions that change the character of the beer, drive off unwanted flavors from the grain, and contribute to the color of the beer. For all-grain brewers, the boil reduces the volume of the wort, concentrating the sugars. A rolling boil is best, and the brew kettle should not be covered or else those unwanted substances that would normally be driven off will be unable to escape from the pot.

Hops are often added in stages during the boil. When the boil first begins, add the hops that will provide bitterness. These should boil for at least one hour. Often brewers will add more hops about 30 to 40 minutes into the boil to provide flavor and again at the very end of the boil to provide aroma.

Cooling the Wort

After the boil is finished, you need to cool the wort before you can add yeast. One way that extract brewers often cool their wort is to begin the brewing by only boiling 6 quarts of water, boiling with the extract and syrup, and then at the end of the boil mixing the hot wort in the fermenter with about 3½ gallons of cold water. This works fairly well except during the summer months when the water is too warm. All-grain brewers will always have at least 5 gallons that need to be chilled, and many extract brewers find that boiling with a full 5-gallon volume can help improve their beers. If you need to cool a large amount of beer, a wort chiller is invaluable.

FERMENTATION

After the wort is cool enough to pitch yeast (usually somewhere in the 60° to 68°F range for ales, but always below 80°), you will want to aerate the wort. One way to do this is to simply shake the fermenter as vigorously as possible, or to splash the wort as you siphon it into the fermenter. Aeration is important because oxygen will help promote vigorous yeast growth.

You then add the yeast, shaking the fermenter or stirring the mixture. Many homebrewers prefer to grow large starters before adding the yeast. It's important to realize that low yeast pitching levels are one of the biggest problems homebrewers face. Using starters can solve that problem. If you're not comfortable with yeast starters and are using only dry yeast, adding 3 or 4 packets of yeast instead of the 1 or 2 that some recipes suggest can also give your yeast a leg up on their growth cycle.

After the yeast is added, seal the fermenter (put the lid on if you have a bucket, or use a cap if you have a carboy), put an airlock in place, and leave the beer alone for several (usually 3 to 5) days. Sometimes, after the initially high level of yeast activity settles down, homebrewers will transfer the beer to a second fermenter so that they can remove the clean beer from sediment and, hopefully, end up with a cleaner-tasting and clearer beer. This process of transferring beer from one fermenter to another is called "racking." After racking, the beer is allowed to continue fermenting. This second stage is referred to by brewers as "secondary fermentation."

PACKAGING

After the beer is finished fermenting, you're ready to put it in bottles or a keg. Most homebrewers start out using bottles because of their low cost and ready availability, but a keg is easier to clean and requires a lot less time to deal with.

If you bottle, you'll need at least 2 cases of bottles (that's 48 bottles) to handle a 5-gallon batch. You'll need to clean and sanitize the bottles and then prime your beer to provide carbonation. Priming is the addition of a small amount of sugar to induce a small second fermentation that produces carbon dioxide. Usually ¾ cup of corn sugar is used. Some homebrewers have added priming sugar by the teaspoon to each bottle, but that's more work than is necessary and produces inconsistent results. It's easier to add the corn sugar to the entire volume of beer, mix it in, and then siphon the beer into the bottles.

Then it is time to cap the bottles, wait about 2 weeks, and enjoy a cool, refreshing homemade beer!

Terms used throughout the text may be unfamiliar to novice homebrewers; therefore a glossary has been added at the end of the book. Suppliers named in the text can be found at the end of the book in the Sources section. The Supplier list is by no means exhaustive, and many of the gadgets described here may be available at lower cost directly from your local homebrew supply shop.

– 1 –

THE HOME BREWERY

EVERY HOMEBREWER HAS DIFFERENT PRIORITIES, constraints, and philosophies. These differences are reflected in the wide range of approaches used in selecting and making homebrewing equipment. Some brewers feel that cost is no object if performance can be boosted even slightly, no matter that the improvement may exist only in the brewer's mind. Others get pleasure in finding ways to do things themselves even if it takes hours or days of effort to save a few dollars. Different folks have different priorities, but in the end all brewers have the same number one priority — making great beer.

Brewing equipment, therefore, has just one purpose: to do its job well, with the goal of producing great beer. For example, mash tuns hold the mash at constant temperatures for prescribed periods of time; filters remove particles of a certain size; and so on. There are often many ways to accomplish any given step, and the way one brewer does something may not be the way another does it. Even experienced brewers disagree about the "best" way to brew. Getting hung up on minor points wastes time and money that could be better spent brewing and drinking, but discussing preferred brewing techniques is fun and a great excuse to get together to drink beer.

In this chapter we introduce a few basic ideas about brewing equipment: what kinds of equipment you need to equip a home brewery, what kinds of equipment are generally used in a small commercial brewery, and how to keep your brewing equipment clean and in good condition.

Equipment for the Home Brewery

The equipment needed to start brewing at home is fairly minimal. You probably already have a large stock pot and a mixing spoon — that takes care of your brew kettle. You'll also need a fermenter, some tubing to move the beer from one place to another, and a way to package the beer, which usually means getting a bottle capper. The investment in equipment is small. Many homebrew supply shops sell basic equipment sets for less than $50. That's what it costs to play the game.

A homebrewing set usually includes:

✔ One 6½ gallon plastic bucket with lid drilled and fitted with a grommet or stopper for an airlock
✔ Plastic airlock
✔ Hydrometer
✔ Bottle brush
✔ Siphon tube
✔ Racking cane
✔ Sanitizer
✔ Introductory book
✔ Bottle capper

Equipment sets do vary. Some may also include a bottle filler, a tube clamp, bottle caps, or upgrades to certain basic equipment. If the set doesn't include a thermometer, you may want

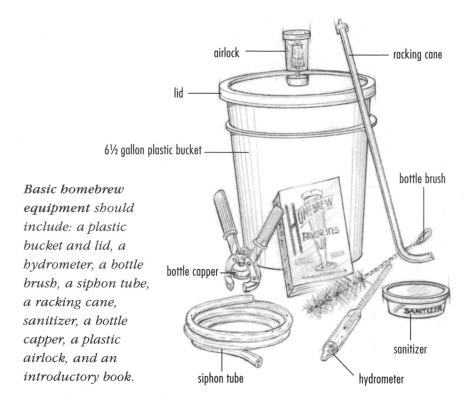

airlock

lid

6½ gallon plastic bucket

racking cane

bottle brush

bottle capper

sanitizer

siphon tube

hydrometer

Basic homebrew equipment should include: a plastic bucket and lid, a hydrometer, a bottle brush, a siphon tube, a racking cane, sanitizer, a bottle capper, a plastic airlock, and an introductory book.

to buy one. You *won't* find a kettle, spoon, or bottles in these basic equipment sets, but other than that, they'll have the items you need to brew your first batch.

For a brewer using recipes based on malt extract, the basic homebrewing set will work fine for quite a while. Eventually you may want to upgrade some of these items, as through your own experience and contact with other homebrewers you become aware of other brewing techniques. Some typical upgrades may include:

✔ Replacing the plastic buckets with a glass carboy, or even a stainless-steel vessel
✔ Replacing the bottle capper with a bench capper
✔ Obtaining funnels and strainers

✔ Replacing the airlock with other models
✔ Upgrading the bottle filler
✔ Buying more books
✔ Using larger bottles, or maybe even investing in kegging equipment

Eventually, you may decide that all-grain recipes aren't too hard (they really aren't), and then you'll need a few more gadgets:

✔ Some sort of mashing and sparging setup (can be built for as little as $15)
✔ A larger pot (unless you've already got one that can boil at least 7 gallons)
✔ A wort chiller (can be built for about $20)

That's really all you need to start mashing — although most homebrewers find that better equipment is easier to use, easier to keep clean, or produces better beer. Once you've really got the homebrew bug, you'll probably want some other equipment. Some items that really can make a difference in the pleasure you get from the hobby include:

✔ Roller malt mill
✔ Kegging equipment
✔ Refrigerator for fermenting and storing beer

Buying homebrewing equipment is a lot like buying cars. The ultimate goal might be to get you from your home to your office. Both a $1,000 clunker and a $250,000 Lamborghini will accomplish that — the choice is yours. It's the same thing with homebrewing equipment. Although you can enter the all-grain brewing game for as little as $50 over your initial equipment investment, there are also some very well built, well designed stainless-steel systems that can easily run you $5,000. And just like the car market, there are products everywhere in between the two extremes. Each does things in different ways, each has its merits and drawbacks, and each has a price tag (either in terms of money or your time). We'll try to guide you around the showrooms, and we'll try to let you know when you can get a better deal elsewhere. Ultimately it's your choice, your money, and your brewery, so weigh the benefits and drawbacks carefully, and use the setup that best suits your needs and your brewing style.

LESSONS FROM THE PROS: EQUIPMENT IN A SMALL COMMERCIAL BREWERY

The processes used in a commercial brewery are similar to those that homebrewers follow. The difference is in scale: Whereas a pot on a stove works fine for a homebrewer, a commercial brewer may have a 900 gallon brew kettle with a gas-fired burner. Let's take a moment to tour a small microbrewery — Brimstone Brewing of Baltimore, Maryland — and look at some of the equipment used there.

The brewing process begins with the malt mill. Brimstone's two-roller mill, typical to those found in many small craft breweries, is similar to the roller mills used by homebrewers except that the hopper is bigger, the rollers are bigger, and there's a chute to carry the milled grain from the mill to the mash tun.

The mash tun, a stainless-steel vessel with a perforated stainless-steel false bottom, is used to mix the grist with hot water and allow the malt enzymes to convert the grain starch to sugar. Some mash tuns have steam-fired heating systems that enable brewers to adjust mash temperatures. The single-step infusion mashing system used in the Brimstone brewery, however, relies on hot water infused from a hot liquor tank to achieve the proper mash temperature (temperatures are shown on a digital control panel). Even though this mash tun is heavily insulated, the sheer mass of the mash likely would retain heat long enough to achieve saccharification (the conversion of starches to sugars) even if there were no insulation.

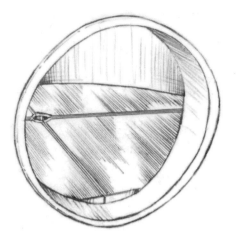

False bottoms are common in commercial small breweries. The slotted false bottom allows sweet liquid to drain across the entire area of the bottom of the grain bed.

At the end of the saccharification period, the mash is sparged with hot water and the sweet liquid is pumped to the brew kettle, which is a 15-barrel stainless-steel vessel with a gas-fired burner. This is similar to setting a modified keg on a propane cooker, but it's more than 30 times larger in scale. (In the brew kettle, the sweet liquid extracted from the grains is boiled and hops are added. At this point we start calling the liquid "wort.")

At the end of the boil, the wort is chilled using a heat exchanger. Homebrewers can accomplish this (achieving a quick drop of temperature in a flow of hot wort) with a counterflow chiller. The heat exchanger used at Brimstone relies on cool water as the heat-absorbing medium and has a fitting for an air stone that allows fresh oxygen to be pumped into the wort as it passes through the heat exchanger. After the wort leaves the exchanger, it is pumped into one of several 30-barrel stainless-steel fermenters.

Depending on the type of beer being produced, the people at Brimstone either use a high-gravity brewing method (in which beer is first brewed to a high gravity and then diluted to a normal gravity to fill the fermenter) or brew twice to fill one fermenter. The fermenters have jackets through which refrigerated glycol (an antifreeze and coolant) is pumped to keep the fermenter cool.

With the Brimstone fermenter setup, the yeast settles to the bottom of the vessel and can be removed from the fermenting beer. This is the idea behind brewing equipment such as the Brewcap inverted carboy fermenter available from BrewCo. It is important to note that the glycol jacket makes it possible to maintain consistent temperature for the fermenting beer. This is critical to achieving consistent product quality. It also illustrates the importance of controlling the temperature range of a fermenting beer — possibly by using a device such as the FermTemp controller from Brewers Resource, which controls not only the lower range of the temperature but the upper range as well.

After fermentation and before going to the keg, the beer runs through a diatomaceous earth (DE) filter for clarity and is pumped to a bright beer tank for conditioning. The bright beer tank holds finished beer that's ready to be carbonated and packaged. As a homebrewer, you can achieve similar clarity and stability with a cartridge or plate-type filter.

One of the things that we can learn from Brimstone Brewing is the importance of moving beer from one vessel to another. The illustration on page 13 shows the

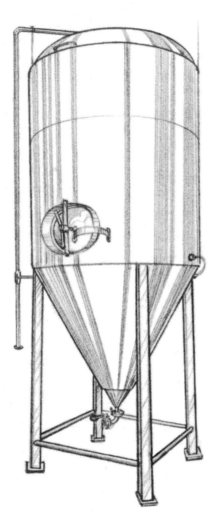

Cylindroconical fermenters, such as this one at Brimstone, circulate refrigerated glycol to reduce the heat and maintain the proper temperature.

connections used in professional brewing equipment. The equipment is fitted with triclamp flanges, and the hoses are connected using triclamp connectors and gaskets. This makes it possible to connect any piece of equipment to a hose and move beer easily from vessel to vessel. Other equipment has quick-disconnect fittings to enable hoses or other equipment to be easily attached, making the brewing process flexible and ultimately

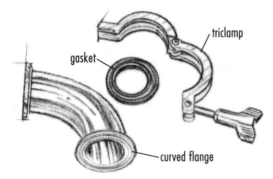

Professional brewers use quick-disconnect fittings such as this triclamp, pictured here with a gasket and flange, to keep the process flexible.

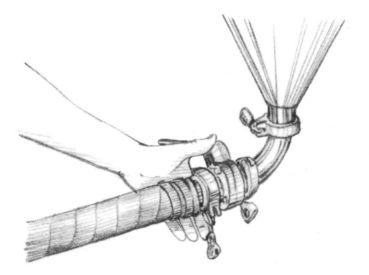

Connecting a hose to a flange with a triclamp is a simple procedure — much easier than traditional plumbing connections.

easier. The lesson here for homebrewers is to consider the flow of material throughout the brewing process and to try to use standard-size fittings for vessel outlets and standard-size hoses throughout your brewery. Doing so will make your equipment easier to use. Consistent use of simple-to-use connections is a good example of how planning ahead can pay benefits in the long run.

Tewey also suggests that homebrewers think about doing a little plumbing. For example, an extra faucet at the right height or point in the brewing process is not beyond the skills of many homebrewers, and it can make brewing considerably easier.

Sanitation is stressed in every homebrewing textbook, and a visit to Brimstone further emphasizes its importance. Hoses and equipment are stored full of iodophor, a sanitizing agent. A large bucket of iodophor solution is available for small parts and fittings; after use, the parts are returned to the sanitizing bucket.

In a small brewery, yeast is reused several times and yeast cultures are maintained and grown as needed. Tewey stresses that maintaining yeasts and growing cultures is easy, ensures proper pitching rates, and is less expensive in the long run than constantly buying yeasts for each batch. In Chapter 12 we discuss the equipment and processes used for cultivating yeast.

SANITATION

Keeping equipment clean and in good repair is an essential part of homebrewing. In fact, most brewers (both professional and amateur) probably spend more time cleaning than brewing. Sanitation is the single most important factor in determining whether your beer turns out great or is completely undrinkable.

You may hear brewers say they are going to "sterilize" their equipment. They're really not sterilizing, which means killing absolutely every microorganism. Actually they're "sanitizing" their equipment, which means that they're sharply reducing the possibility of microorganisms existing on the surfaces of their brewing equipment.

Sanitation is most often accomplished by using solutions of various chemical sanitizing agents. The agents most commonly used by homebrewers include: chlorine bleach, oxidizers (e.g., B-Brite), iodophor, and trisodium phosphate (TSP). Equipment can also be sanitized by using heat: either by boiling in water or by baking in an oven, which is essentially what an autoclave does. Of course you need to be aware of the temperature range that your equipment can withstand.

Homebrewers often use chlorine as a sanitizer, but it is very corrosive to metals and should never be left in contact with stainless-steel equipment for any period of time. If your stainless-steel equipment does come in contact with chlorine, rinse it well with clean water immediately.

> Do not mix any sanitizers with other household cleaners; some mixtures, such as ammonia and chlorine, can create dangerous gases.

One of the best sanitizers available to homebrewers who use stainless-steel equipment is iodophor, a solution of 1.75 percent iodine and 18.75 percent phosphoric acid. Iodophor does not corrode stainless-steel equipment and is often left in unused equipment to keep it sanitary. Further, iodophor does not require extensive rinsing. After soaking equipment in an iodophor solution, simply air dry the equipment and it is ready for use — although rinsing is still often done to avoid possible off flavors.

Some homebrewers are concerned about introducing waterborne bacteria to sanitized equipment by rinsing with water, so they air dry after soaking in iodophor. Our view is that air drying alone means that the equipment is sitting out for long periods of time and runs a small risk of airborne contaminants adhering to it. So either way, some risk is involved; but it's minimal and not worth the worry. Iodophor is available in small bottles from homebrew supply shops for a couple of dollars. It is sometimes available in 1-gallon jugs from restaurant supply businesses. It is also available in rural areas at feed stores, where it is sold as "Tank Cleaner" in 1-gallon jugs at prices that are not much more than homebrewers pay for a few ounces. Avoid the types sold as "udder wash" or "teet clean," as they often contain lanolin.

Trisodium phosphate (TSP) is an industrial cleaner that is sometimes available from paint suppliers, but your local hardware store is likely to have it as well. Painters use TSP to remove wallpaper and clean equipment. If you use TSP as a sanitizer, be sure to rinse the equipment with clean water after contact with the TSP solution.

Alcohol can also be used to sanitize equipment. Some brewers keep a small sprayer of a diluted alcohol solution handy to spray down small areas. Brewers who culture yeast often use alcohol or heat to sterilize equipment and surfaces. Use ethanol, either vodka or grain alcohol. For culturing equipment, we use full strength grain alcohol. For general sanitation we use 20 percent alcohol, which is vodka diluted with water in a 1:1 ratio, or grain alcohol in water at a 1:5 ratio.

Vinegar is acetic acid; using white vinegar right out of the bottle will effectively clean copper utensils such as chilling coils. Phosphoric acid can also be used. This is often available from farm supply stores as dairy acid rinse.

Remember: Sanitize your equipment well before use, and again before storing it.

Although all your equipment should be clean, it is vitally important that you sanitize well those items that are used after the boil. Mashing vessels, boiling vessels, spoons, paddles, and similar items should be clean, but meticulous sanitation of these items is significantly less critical than sanitation of fermenters, chillers, airlocks, hydrometers, or anything that touches chilled wort.

– 2 –

BUILDING A HOME BREWERY

IN THIS CHAPTER WE DESCRIBE SOME OF THE FACTORS and considerations that go into setting up a dedicated brewery area in your home, be it a corner of the basement, a shed, or the back of a garage. If you're brewing with basic equipment in a kitchen and are happy with that setup, then by all means skip this chapter; but if you're thinking about setting aside a good, workable area to use for a long time, this chapter will suggest ways to make your home brewery work better for you.

MATERIALS FOR FABRICATING EQUIPMENT

Most homebrewing equipment is made of metal, plastic, or glass. In this section we briefly review the pros and cons of each material and highlight certain factors to keep in mind when working with or selecting these materials. Generally, avoid using materials that are not recognized as safe for use with food or drinking water if those materials will be in contact with your beer.

Plastic

Plastics are used in a wide range of brewing equipment, from the plastic buckets that many of us used for fermenting our first batch, to hoses for siphons or keg lines, to highly durable plastics such as the newly available Lexan fermenters. Plastic is a useful material for many home brewery applications. It's light, inexpensive, flexible, and also resists breaking, but it needs to be used with a little common sense.

There are a number of factors to consider when choosing equipment made of plastic, the most important of which is whether the plastic is safe for use with food products. Some plastics leach chemicals, known as plasticizers, to any liquid that is stored or passed through them. This is especially true of PVC, which does come in food-grade varieties. So when you're buying plastic hoses, buckets, pipes, or containers, make sure they are intended for food preparation. Ask if the plastic is "FDA approved" or "NSF approved." If it's not, you may want to avoid using it to store anything you're planning to drink.

If you're using a plastic hose for transferring hot wort, you'll want to consider its operating temperature range. Many vinyl hoses (actually made of PVC) used by homebrewers are intended for temperatures up to about 160°F. Above that, they begin to collapse.

Some homebrewers have used schedule 40 PVC pipes, such as those used in household plumbing, to build certain homebrewing equipment. Not all PVC pipe is safe to use in food contact areas, however. If you're shopping around, ask the supplier if it's safe for use as hot-water supply lines. If it is, then it should be safe for use in brewing equipment. If it's not recommended for that use, then you're better off not using it in any of your equipment. The chlorinated PVC (CPVC) is often used for water supply lines, and we're unaware of problems associated with use of this pipe in brewing equipment. The rule here is this: If you are in doubt about an item, ask someone. We've found that once you explain that you need something for homebrewing, generally the reaction will be very positive. Don't be surprised if the guy at your local hardware store starts asking you questions about homebrewing. If so, recruit him to the legions of the homebrewing army.

Plastic fermenters are usually made of polyethylene, which comes in two types: high density (HDPE) and low density (LDPE). The HDPE is more durable and stands up better to heat. Both types are prone to scratching, which is often believed to harbor bacteria that can infect the beer. If you're using plastic vessels, you may want to treat them gently, examine them periodically for signs of scratching, and replace them promptly.

Glass

Glass fermenters are easily cleaned, inexpensive, and very durable. They can be sanitized by extended soaking of several hours or days in chlorine solutions and are commonly used throughout the homebrewing community. (In fact, glass fermenters are often stored full of sanitizing solution when not in use.) The only downside of glass that we're aware of is that it sometimes breaks. The necks of glass carboys are fragile, and lifting them by the neck is not recommended. Besides the obvious danger of dropping a carboy, glass will fracture when faced with temperature stress. Pouring hot water or wort into a carboy is never a good idea, nor is applying heat directly to a carboy. We've heard from one homebrewer who set a hot glass carboy in a snowbank to cool. You'll waste a lot of carboys with this trick!

Stainless Steel

Stainless steel is one of the best materials for most homebrewing equipment. It's durable, withstands heat, and is easily sanitized. The one thing to be aware of is that stainless steel can be damaged by extended contact with chlorine-based sanitizers. Filling a brewpot with a bleach-water solution and soaking equipment in it is not recommended. Iodophor is a good sanitizer for stainless steel.

Copper

Copper is used by homebrewers most often for chiller coils and racking tubes. Historically it's been the material of choice for use in brew kettles; but given their high cost, copper brew kettles are a rarity today. It's a good idea, however, to use some piece of copper equipment in the boil because it provides nutrients for the yeast. Some brewers have a small piece of copper tubing that they drop into the kettle for this purpose. Copper also reacts with chlorine sanitizers; therefore, copper equipment should not be left to soak in chlorine solutions for extended periods. Copper can be cleaned effectively with white distilled vinegar.

Aluminum

Aluminum is a good material for many brewing applications. It will work fine for a brew kettle or for heating sparge water. There is no problem with beers picking up off flavors from the metal or from worts reacting in any way with the aluminum. However, chlorine-based sanitizers are likely to corrode aluminum equipment.

Other Metals

Brewers often use bronze or brass fittings for brew kettles. These metals resist the acidity of wort reasonably well, but they generally react with chlorine-based sanitizers. Be aware that brass contains some lead to improve machineability. When cutting, sanding, grinding, or otherwise working brass, a thin film of lead can be deposited on the brass. This can be removed with a 2:1 solution of white vinegar and hydrogen peroxide. (It is also possible that at some time in the future, the FDA will issue warnings against using brass with food.)

Solders are a mixed blessing. They are needed to seal joints between pipes and fittings, but some contain metals that can leach into the wort. Soft solders usually have low melting temperatures of around 450°F and come in two types: a mixture of tin and lead, which you don't want to use in your home brewery; or lead-free solder, which is required by law for use in drinking water systems and works fine with most brewing equipment. Lead-free solder is great for soldering copper, but it will not work with stainless steel. For stainless-steel equipment you will need to use silver solder.

Even though lead-free soft solder contains 2 percent silver, it should not be confused with silver solder. Silver solder requires much higher temperatures — over 800°F — and will work with stainless steel. Unfortunately, silver solders can contain numerous different metals, one of which is cadmium. This is something you don't want in your brews — or anywhere else, for that matter. So if your package of silver solder does not provide an analysis of its contents, don't buy it. Take your items to a welding shop and discuss your needs with them. They should have the right material.

Wood

The only uses for wood in the home brewery that we know of are for wooden paddles for stirring the mash, wooden stands for setting up a tiered brewery structure, and incidental items such as carboy carts. When working with wood, remember:

✔ Wood is flammable, so setting a 200,000 BTU burner on top of it may not be wise.
✔ Pressure-treated lumber is treated with chemicals that you don't want to have near food-preparation surfaces. Use common sense.

DESIGNING YOUR HOME BREWERY

An ideal home brewery would be built as a special room in the house or in a dedicated space (such as part of the basement or garage) where every aspect of the brewery is built in from the start: there should be adequate natural gas and electric lines, air vents, plumbing, and even a sloped concrete floor with embedded drainage. In reality, many constraints are placed on most home breweries, especially in terms of space and costs. If you are fortunate enough to be building a new home, though, sneak a brewery design into the plans, build it, and then call us to come and taste the results of your labor while we tell you how cool your brewery looks.

There are almost as many homebrewing equipment setups as there are brewers. The key point to remember when designing your home brewery is to be flexible. As your skill level increases, your appetite for new equipment or different approaches is also likely to increase, not just because you move up to more advanced techniques but because you may become less willing to accept compromises. Therefore, as you work on developing the design for your home brewery, it's important to plan for future growth.

Breweries, as a rule, need to be scrupulously clean to reduce the chances of unwanted bacteria taking up residence. So you should focus on how you'll keep the brewery clean even before you set it up. Two factors to consider are your work surfaces and the floors. Choose materials for work surfaces that will not easily harbor microorganisms; smooth metal or tile are good. These can easily be wiped clean, sprayed with chlorine solution, and therefore remain clean. If possible, select a floor that can be hosed down. Doubtless this will be impossible if you're working in your kitchen; but a floor with a slight slope and a drain, such as the concrete floor in your basement or garage, would allow you to spray everything with a sanitizing solution and hose it down after brewing.

Don't Fight Gravity

The classic design of a brewery is what is known as the "tower arrangement." The idea is to keep liquids and solids moving in a downward direction throughout the brewing process so that you don't have to pump liquids or lift materials. Remember, a gallon of wort weighs almost 8½ pounds, and most homebrewers brew batches of 5, 10, or 15 gallons. This means you'll be dealing with volumes of liquids weighing anywhere from 40 to 150 pounds, excluding the weight of the kettle, the weight of soggy grains, and so forth. When you design your brewery, think about gravity. Keep in mind how liquids and solids move from one step to the next, and try to keep things moving downhill. Take advantage of natural flows and siphons as much as possible.

When we talk about utility, we're talking about ease of use more than anything else. Keeping things close together (but not so close that you're cramped) makes a lot of sense. You certainly don't want to be doing your mash in the kitchen and then carrying a 70-pound kettle through the house, across the front porch, and over to the driveway where you set up your propane burner. There are a number of things to consider when you set up your brewery.

Proximity. Keep your equipment as close together as you can, but avoid crowding.

Height. Gravity can work for you, making it easy to move from one step to another; but if you have to lift grains and liquids over your head to accomplish this, you've taken the concept too far.

Flow. Consider the order in which brewing steps are carried out. Try to organize your equipment in such a way that you take advantage of the flow.

Ventilation. If you're using a propane or other gas burner to heat water and wort, make sure that you've got adequate air flow. Using propane cookers indoors is not a good idea. Even in a garage, make sure you leave the door open.

Power. You'll need power for lighting, pumps (if you use them), and electric heating elements or stoves. Some electric brew buckets require 220-volt power supplies; remember that when you decide where to place your brewery. When setting up your power supply, keep in mind that the brewery is an area where you will be working with liquids and possibly spilling pools of water or beer. Make sure you install a ground-fault circuit interrupt (GFCI) in the brewery area for your own safety. Either a dedicated circuit with a GFCI breaker in the box or a GFCI electric outlet as the first outlet in the circuit will work fine. If you're not comfortable working with electricity, get a professional electrician to do this for you.

Water. Even if you're using bottled or pre-boiled water, you still need a source of water for cleaning, chilling (if you use wort chillers), and possible other uses. In addition to the water supply, you need a place to drain waste water. A laundry tub works for many homebrewers, although a floor drain is fine too.

Of course, you'll need to balance these factors against cost, space, and choices you've already made in selecting various pieces of equipment. There's not one right way to set up a home brewery. As long as the setup works for you and makes good beer, you should feel perfectly happy to violate any guideline that we (or any other homebrewer) might suggest. More extensive discussions of home brewery design are available in an excellent article by Jim Busch in the January/February 1995 issue of *Brewing Techniques*.

One other consideration is the question of whether it's better to buy or to make any particular piece of equipment. Again, this is your call. Some equipment is difficult to make, some requires special expertise that not everyone possesses, and some is just too costly or impractical to build at home. Throughout this book we try to strike a balance between building things ourselves and buying things that aren't practical to build. Oftentimes it's cheaper to buy something than to build it, even if building it isn't difficult. At other times the investment of a few extra dollars gives you a better-made gadget. It's your brewery and your skills that we're talking about, so you make the call.

BREWERY DESIGNS THAT WORK

Like everything in brewing, the subject of brewery design is one of balance. You want an easy-to-use setup that takes advantage of process flow and gravity to give you an efficient system that produces great beers. In this section we discuss a few options that have worked for many homebrewers. Feel free to adopt them or adapt them as you see fit.

The Classic Tower Design

The classic tower design, mentioned earlier, has been used for centuries if not millennia. It starts with the grain on the highest level of the brewery, where it's milled and sent down a chute into the mash tun. From there, the mash is lautered (run off and sparged) and the liquid is piped down a level to the brew kettle. After the boil, the hot wort is chilled and sent down another level to the fermenter.

This simple use of gravity flow occurs in many homebrewer setups found in garages and basements around the world. It's also embodied in some of the most state-of-the-art setups sold today as "turnkey" systems by homebrewing equipment vendors. For example, the three-vessel systems sold by Brewers Warehouse are intended to be used in a classic tower, gravity-flow setup, even though the systems themselves do not come with the necessary stands. You can follow the instructions below to build your own stand that will work well with this type of setup. (Pico-Brewing Systems of Ypsilanti, Michigan, sells tiered stands for gravity-flow brewing setups. See Suppliers, page 241, for addresses.)

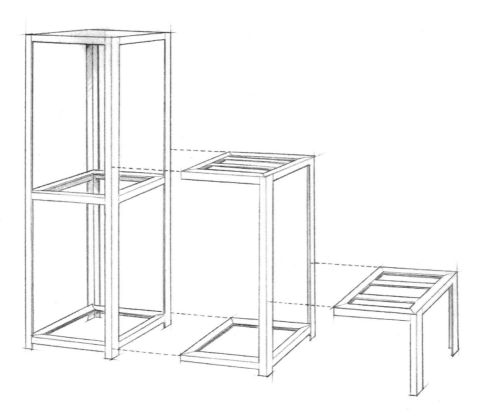

*You can build a **three-level stand** out of metal for a classic gravity-flow tower system. Modify this basic design to fit your own needs.*

Building a Tower Brewery Stand

The stand is best set up in a permanent location. Using modified kegs as brew vessels, the overall dimensions are 7 feet high by 4½ feet wide by 1½ feet deep. Construct it from 1-inch angle iron, or use uni-struts (steel angles with pre-drilled holes) if you do not have access to a welder. The top level should be 5 feet high, the second level 36 inches high, and the bottom level about 12 inches off the ground. The width and length of each level of the platform will depend on the size of your brewing equipment. Generally, for modified kegs, about 18 inches square will work for the shelves. Widen the middle level for the longer dimension of picnic-cooler mash tun.

Make sure you have a small stepstool for filling the top pot, as you do not want to lift a full pot to that height. This is a good application for a pump. If you wish, a single, large propane tank can be strapped onto the outside of the frame instead of messing about with two or three bottles. Indeed, there may be a substantial savings on propane costs in doing this. Many places charge a flat rate for filling a 20-pound bottle, regardless of how much is left in the tank. If you brew many batches, it may be a better idea to connect to a large outdoor propane tank and really save some money.

Materials for Tower Brewery Stand

Legs

Four 60" x 1" lengths of angle iron
Two 36" x 1" lengths of angle iron
Two 12" x 1" lengths of angle iron

Shelf supports

Twenty-four 18" x 1" lengths of angle iron with ends
    cut to 45 degrees

Cooker shelf cross member

Six 17¾" x 1" lengths of angle iron

Shelves for propane bottles

Three 18" square sections of expanded aluminum or steel

Heat shields

Two 18" x 24" long thin aluminum sheets
Three low-profile 125,000 BTU cookers with bolting brackets
    on bottom (Camp Chef — Low Profile)

Directions

1. Cut out all materials as indicated above.
2. Assemble four shelf supports into a square. Square up and weld together. Repeat for a total of six shelf supports.
3. Select three shelf frames for the top cooker shelves.
4. Measure the distance between the bolt holes on the cookers. Add 1 to this number and subtract from 18. Divide by 2. Measure in this distance from the ends, and set two cross members at this point and weld. Do the same for the other two shelves.
5. Set the cookers in the center of one of the shelves, mark the mounting holes onto the frame, and drill holes into the cross members. Do the same for the other two shelves. (Do not mount the cookers yet.)
6. Clamp the 60" legs onto one of the cooker shelves and weld.
7. Clamp a propane bottle shelf 1 inch from the bottom of the 60" legs and weld.
8. Clamp and weld a second propane shelf 28 inches from the top of the bottom shelf.
9. Clamp and weld the two 36" legs onto another cooker shelf.
10. Clamp the last propane shelf 1 inch from the bottom of the 36" legs and weld.
11. Weld middle shelf assembly to the first shelf assembly.
12. Clamp the two 12" legs onto the last cooker shelf and weld into place.
13. Weld this short shelf assembly onto the main shelf assembly.
14. Bolt one propane cooker onto each of the cooker shelves (top shelves).

(more on page 30)

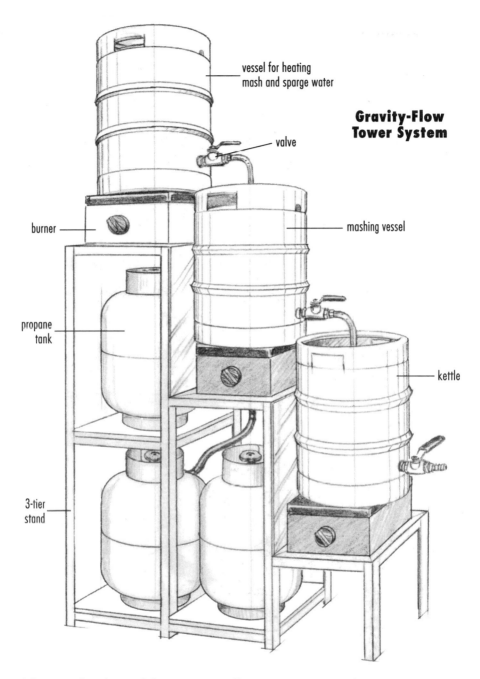

Gravity-Flow Tower System

vessel for heating mash and sparge water

valve

burner

mashing vessel

propane tank

kettle

3-tier stand

*The completed stand for a **gravity-flow tower system:** As you can see, it is best set up in an extremely well-ventilated location.*

15. Using either screws or pop rivets, attach a heat shield to the legs next to the center cooker; then do the same for the bottom cooker. These prevent the bottles of propane from getting too hot.

16. Put the expanded metal sections on the propane-bottle shelf frames. These sections do not need to be anchored to the frames, but you can do so if you wish.

17. Set the assembly in its permanent home.

18. Add propane bottles, and connect them to the cookers. *Check for gas leaks at all connections!* (A mixture of dish soap and water applied to each connection will bubble if there is a gas leak.) Leaks can be sealed with Teflon tape.

19. Add kettles, and you're ready to brew.

Note: If you have to take this to a professional welder and he makes some recommendations that are different than those stated here, please listen to him. He may suggest improvements that could strengthen the system.

Many homebrewers use other types of mashing vessels, such as picnic coolers with manifolds. These, too, are easily adapted to the gravity-flow tower model. Simply put a burner and a pot for heating water on the top level. Put the cooler mash tun, complete with sparge apparatus, on the second level; then run a tube from the hot-water pot to the sparge apparatus. Finally, drain the mash tun directly into a brew kettle on the lower level.

To build such a stand, assemble the large- and small-shelf stands as described in the gravity-flow tower system. The center shelf will need to be 28 inches wide for a 48-quart cooler, or 36 inches wide for an 80-quart cooler. As you will not be adding the low-profile cooker to this shelf, the stand will also need to be 6 to 8 inches taller, depending on the style of cooker used. Weld this center stand to the tall and short stands. Be sure to use a heat shield next to the burner to prevent melting the cooler.

Gravity-Flow Tower

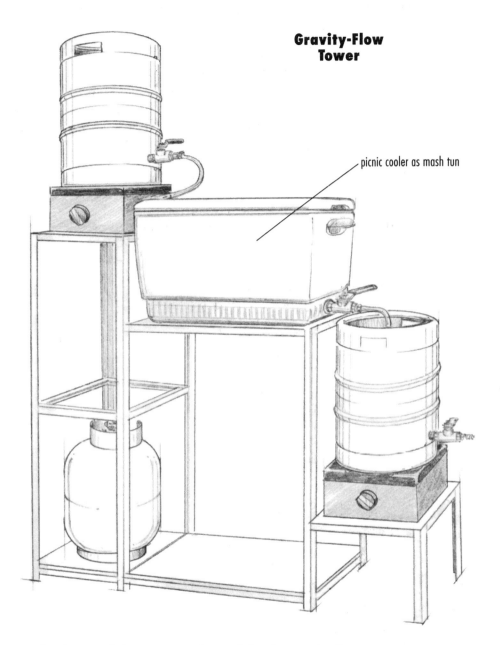

picnic cooler as mash tun

*The design of the **three-level stand** for the gravity-flow tower can be altered for use with a picnic-cooler mash tun.*

The Beer Tree

The idea of minimizing the amount of space taken up by the brewing setup, while still taking advantage of downward gravity flow, was discussed by Dave O'Neil in the March/April 1994 issue of *Brewing Techniques*. The idea is to build a structure on which the various pieces of brewing apparatus can be stacked one above the other along the sides of a vertical stand.

The structure O'Neil built was made from 14-gauge box steel with a 6-foot length of 2-inch by 2-inch steel as the main upright pole. Dave also built the base of 2-inch by 2-inch steel. The base is 3 feet across the center length and 2 feet across the foot lengths. The support arms were built of 1½-inch by 1½-inch steel.

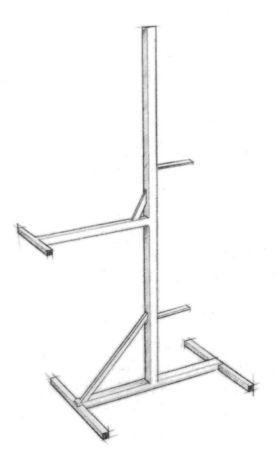

The Beer Tree frame.
It originally appeared in "Beer Tree: A Three-Tiered System with Roots in Simplicity," by Dave O'Neil, Brewing Techniques *2 (2), (1994).*

A support brace from the bottom of the stand to the vertical up-right was built of 1-inch by 1-inch steel and welded at a 45-degree angle. All the pieces were welded together.

An interesting variation on the tree stand is a ladder-like setup with three levels for the hot-liquor bath, the mash tun, and a wort-collection vessel. The boil would have to be done elsewhere, usually on a nearby propane burner. Listermann Manufacturing used this type of setup to display its Phil's Lautering System at the 1995 American Homebrewers Association (AHA) conference. The stand is not widely available. Ask at your homebrew shop.

Listermann built the stand of wood, using 1½-inch by 1½-inch or 2-inch by 2-inch lumber for the four support pieces and 1-inch by 3-inch lumber for three platforms, all on a base of 1½-inch by ½-inch wood.

See Suppliers, page 241, for sources of brewery equipment.

– 3 –

TOOLS

IN THIS CHAPTER WE EXAMINE an assortment of gadgets, testing devices, and other accessories that make brewing easier, more predictable, and more fun. We begin with a discussion of testing equipment because most homebrewers use these items. Then we look at simple gadgets that you might not have encountered before. Next we discuss filters and pumps, which are occasionally used in homebrewing. Finally we mention containers that can be used to store extra ingredients.

TESTING AND MONITORING

All brewers need to measure temperature and density, so in this section we examine the use of thermometers and hydrometers. In addition, because all-grain brewers need to measure the acidity of their wort, we describe pH meters and how they are used.

Thermometers and Temperature Measurement

The brewer's single most important testing device is the thermometer. Knowing the right temperature is critical to effective mashing and yeast pitching; and in fact, at each step throughout the brewing process, the homebrewer must know the exact temperature.

There are a wide range of thermometers available to the homebrewer. Simple glass cooking thermometers work well for most purposes. Many homebrew suppliers also sell metal cooking thermometers with large, easy-to-read dials on the top. We prefer these, but if you are happy with glass thermometers, there is no reason to switch. You can also buy digital thermometers. In our view their higher cost makes them unattractive, and contrary to what some brewers believe, a digital thermometer is not necessarily any more accurate than either a dial or a glass thermometer.

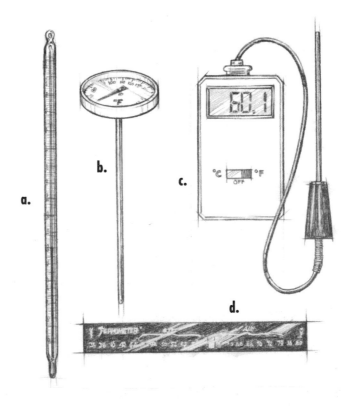

Thermometers vary from traditional to high-tech: a. Glass, b. dial, c. digital, and d. the Fermometer.

Some homebrewers also like to mount thermometers on their mashing vessels and fermenters. For monitoring fermentation temperatures, we like the Fermometer, an adhesive-backed plastic strip thermometer made by Tkach Enterprises (see Suppliers, page 241) that you simply tape to your carboy. These are available at most homebrew supply shops, and you should ask for them at your local store. To make life even easier, the Fermometer's scale is marked with optimal fermentation ranges for both lagers and ales. In our view these strips are an excellent way to monitor the temperature of a carboy without having to insert a thermometer in the liquid or draw off samples. Fermometers are inexpensive, and they are available at supply shops everywhere.

Keep in mind, though, that whereas monitoring the temperature of a fermenter is useful, it's really the control that you need. Ideally you want something that not only measures the temperature but also acts to correct the environment if the temperature goes beyond optimal bounds. For this reason, many homebrewers use refrigerators or freezers with thermostats to actually control the temperature, rather than just monitoring it with thermometers. We discuss using refrigerators, thermostats, and similar solutions on pages 131 to 135.

Hydrometers and Density Measurement

Hydrometers are used to measure the specific gravity, or density, of your beer, which in turn reflects the amount of sugar that has dissolved into the brewing water. By accurately measuring the specific gravity, you can determine (1) when the yeast has finished fermenting, and (2) the amount of alcohol in the final product. Specific gravity can also be important for other reasons, such as calculating hop utilization (the percentage of alpha acids that is isomerized and remains in the finished beer).

When you look for a hydrometer, check the scales on it to make sure that it's calibrated in the same units that you typically use in your brewing. Although many professional brewers and advanced homebrewers prefer to work with the Plato scale, most homebrewers prefer the specific-gravity scale. Many hydrometers also include potential-alcohol scales. (All of these scales are simply different ways of measuring the amount of sugar dissolved in water — think of it as a ruler with inches on one side and centimeters on the other.) The illustration here shows how these scales correlate.

Hydrometers come with a tube that holds the liquid you intend to measure. If you want to pay an extra dollar or so, you can get a more precise hydrometer with a thinner tube so that you can more clearly read the density values.

Although quite a few homebrewers take readings by simply dropping the hydrometer into the wort, it is better to get in the practice of using the hydrometer tube. "Okay," says the novice brewer, "how do I get the beer out of the fermenter and into the tube?" Use a turkey baster or wine thief. Wine thiefs are simple devices with a longer tube than a turkey baster. They do the same thing as a turkey baster, but the longer tube is better suited for removing samples. If you already have a turkey baster, you can extend its reach by attaching a length of vinyl tubing to the end of it.

*Your **hydrometer** should look something like this. Most homebrewers measure density using the specific gravity scale. The Plato scale is another way to measure density. And many hydrometers also include a potential alcohol scale.*

Specific Gravity	Potential Alcohol by Volume	°Plato or Balling
0.990		
1.000	0	0
1.005		1
1.010	1	2
1.015	2	3
		4
1.020	3	5
1.025		6
1.030	4	7
		8
1.035	5	9
1.040		10
1.045	6	11
1.050	7	12
1.055		13
1.060	8	14
		15
1.065	9	16
1.070		17
1.075	10	18
1.080	11	19
1.085		20
1.090	12	21
1.095		22
1.100	13	23
		24
1.105	14	25
1.110		26
1.115	15	27
1.120	16	28

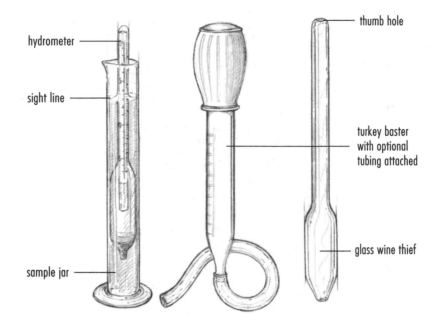

hydrometer

sight line

sample jar

thumb hole

turkey baster
with optional
tubing attached

glass wine thief

*To use your **hydrometer**, you will first need to draw a sample of your beer, and the best ways to do that are to use a **turkey baster** or a glass **wine thief**.*

One thing to keep in mind when using a hydrometer is that it is precise at only one temperature — generally 60°F. However, at 80°F, which is the highest temperature at which you're likely to take a reading, the difference is only 0.002, an inconsequential difference.

pH Meters

Homebrewers who mash their own grains also need to monitor the acidity (pH) of their mash to make sure it stays in the range at which enzymes most effectively convert starches to sugars — a pH of 5.4 to 5.6.

There are two tools commonly used to measure the pH of mash: test strips and digital meters. Test strips are readily available, inexpensive, and easy to use. For a couple of dollars you get a tube of about 100 strips. The inexpensive strips do suffer from inaccuracy (or, rather, imprecision), but there are more expensive strips that will more precisely measure the acidity of your wort. To take a pH reading, draw off a small sample of liquid (no more than an ounce) and set the strip into the liquid. Then discard the liquid (do not pour it back into the mash) and look at the color of the strip. Compare that color with the color bar printed on the tube label to get your test results.

Some of the more advanced homebrewers who love gadgets seem to like pH meters, but we generally find them temperamental, expensive, and complicated to use. These meters are available from some suppliers for as little as $35, although better models can cost twice that. Note that in addition to the pH meter you will need to buy a buffering solution to calibrate the meter. Finally, with pH meters you will very likely need to monitor the temperature of the mash and use a chart to determine a temperature-correction factor, because pH varies with temperature.

Accordingly, our recommendation is to avoid pH meters and use the inexpensive strips. Whereas professional brewers may feel compelled to know the acidity of their mash to a high degree of accuracy, homebrewers just need to know that they're in the ballpark — and the inexpensive strips will do that. If you really have to have a digital pH meter, American Brewmaster has one with an accuracy of 0.1 pH that sells for about $39.

Starch Conversion

One other thing you may want to measure is the conversion of starches to sugars, so that you know when you are done mashing. This can be accomplished easily with a simple iodine test. Many homebrew supply shops sell iodine test strips, which are inexpensive and as easy to use as pH test strips. You may also hear homebrewers talk about the Dextrocheck kit, which was once sold by pharmacists to diabetics. However, with medical advances in recent years, better technology is available to the diabetic and Dextrocheck kits are rarely seen today.

Measuring Color

The spectrophotometer is a nifty gadget that large commercial brewers use to measure color. It measures the light absorbed by a solution — in this case, beer. Human color perception is imprecise, and precisely knowing the color of a homebrew is of questionable value. However, if you are worried about knowing the color of your beer or are trying to reproduce a certain color, you can compare a sample of your beer to a known standard. You might try the standard color slides from Davison Manufacturing. These accurately display colors on the Standard Reference Method (SRM) scale. They give a good eyeball approximation and cost less than $10. These are available at most better homebrew shops.

GADGETS

Funnels can be used whenever you want to pour a liquid from one container to another. Usually homebrewers use large funnels for filling carboys, but a well-equipped home brewery may have several sizes ranging from small funnels for filling bottles or kegs to large funnels for transferring wort to carboys. Some homebrew suppliers also sell snap-in screens for funnels that filter the liquid during transfer. If you can't find the snap-in screens, you may want to look for small strainers that fit inside the funnels. These are useful for filtering out hops when you pour the wort from the pot to the fermenter.

Siphons are simply plastic tubes through which liquid moves by means of a vacuum. Yet homebrewers often worry about how to start the suction. One neat solution is a check valve inserted in the tube. Listermann Manufacturing has such a valve called Phil's Psyphon Starter, which creates a vacuum by simply shaking the hose.

Hooks for the walls or ceiling are simple, and perhaps obvious, gadgets that a lot of brewers overlook. They are great for storing equipment or air drying sanitized hoses or chillers. By hanging the devices, you can keep them out of contact with other surfaces — and out of the way. Don't overlook the simple.

PUMPS

There are several stages in the brewing process when a pump might be handy. In many of these cases you can easily transfer liquid (either water or beer) with a siphon, letting gravity do the work for you. If you have a keg setup, you can also move liquid between vessels under CO_2 pressure. In either case, you can avoid the added expense of a pump with a little planning and ingenuity.

Okay. So you don't want to save money by using gravity or CO_2 to move liquid. You really want a pump. Then you need to consider how you are going to use it. If you will be using the pump to move beer, it will have to be food-grade, allowing no contact between the liquid and any oily machine parts. If you will be using it to move hot wort, make sure it can withstand temperatures of at least 190°F. If you will be using it to move liquid between your mash tun and your boiler, it will have to withstand temperatures of at least 175°F.

For some purposes, such as pumping cold water through an immersion chiller, the type of pump doesn't matter much. Utility pumps and sump pumps are inexpensive and will work fine for these purposes. For moving wort, you'll probably need to spend quite a bit more to get a pump with a magnetic impeller. These are available from places such as Brewers Warehouse.

FILTERS

Although most homebrewers seem content to drink their beer with a bit of sediment in the bottle, others are experimenting with filtering their beer. Filtering produces a very clear beer, with no sediment at the end of the bottle. The most useful application of filters in the home brewery is the use of charcoal filters to remove chlorine from brewing water. Reverse osmosis filters are not generally recommended because they also remove ions from the water, but advanced brewers experimenting with water chemistry may find reverse osmosis filters ideal. Several types of filters are commonly used today; two of the more popular types are (1) cartridge filters with replaceable filter elements, and (2) plate filters with replaceable filter pads. Both systems use CO_2 pressure to move the beer through the filter.

Whichever type of filter you choose, you will have to decide on its granularity, or coarseness. In essence, the finer the holes in the filter, the more material it will remove from the beer. Typical filter sizes used by homebrewers are 5 micron, 2 micron, 1 micron, and 0.5 micron. The larger the number, the more material will pass through. Remember, finer filters have slower flow rates because they retain more of the solid matter. Another consideration is the ease of cleaning. Some filters can be backwashed. Others must be cleaned with caustic solutions.

Cartridge filters consist of a canister, usually made of plastic, into which the filter element is inserted. You can buy stainless-steel canisters, but they are extremely expensive and offer little benefit to the homebrewer. Plastic canisters are available for between $20 and $30, and filter elements cost between $20 and $40.

The Filter Store sells a filter kit specifically designed for homebrewers; however, the filter element included with this kit is a 0.5-micron filter, which is too fine for most homebrews in our opinion — but if you really want brilliant clarity, 0.5 micron will surely give it to you. The Filter Store also offers the kit with

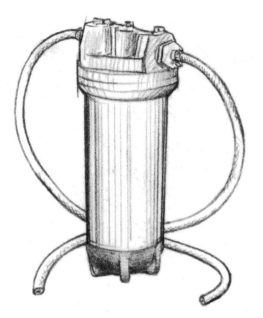

Cartridge filter systems, complete *with plastic canister and replaceable filter inserts, can be used to remove sediment from your beer.*

1-micron and 5-micron filters. We recommend the 5-micron or 2-micron filter for most homebrewers because this will leave behind some yeast.

Generally, a 5-micron filter will get out large residue, such as hops particles and some yeast. At the 1 to 2 micron level, most yeast is removed. At 0.5 micron, all yeast is removed as well as chill haze. At 0.2 micron, bacteria is removed as well as much of the flavor and color.

A more complex, but more flexible, approach for many homebrewers is to use a plate-filter system such as those sold by Marcon Filters. These systems allow you to set up a sequence of filters to remove different sizes of suspended material in a given order. For instance, with this setup you can filter out the coarser material before the liquid reaches a fine filter that would otherwise clog quickly.

The Marcon filter pads range from grades of 00 (very coarse) to 7 (very fine). Marcon filters start at $209 for a 3-plate system (you'll probably want the pressurized system for $215 for

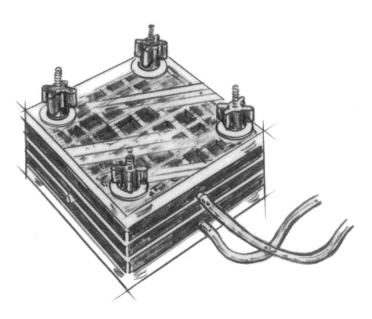

Plate filters can be set up in series to remove virtually all sediment and impurities. Beer is forced under pressure through the sheets, which remove the yeast and haze particles.

3 plates, or $285 for 5 plates). A 5-plate setup with two grades of filters will give you good performance for larger batches. Replacement pads start at about $1. Larger plate units are also available for brewers who can never have too many toys. Some of the larger models sold by Marcon will hold up to 20 plates.

CONTAINERS

After brewing, you'll want to save unused ingredients for upcoming batches. This is especially important once you get a few batches under your belt and start buying ingredients in bulk to save money. All-grain brewers usually buy malt in 50-pound sacks, and one of the most important factors in producing quality beer is to keep the grain dry and free of pests and debris.

Similarly, buying hops in 1-pound or larger bags can yield real cost savings, but you'll want to be able to store the sealed bags in a freezer between batches.

For storing grains, we've found that large plastic bins with snap-on lids, such as those sold by Rubbermaid, work very well. You may want a large bin for your base grist (pale malt) and several small bins, or Tupperware bowls, for storing specialty grains, of which you may only need to store a half-pound or so between batches.

For storing hops in the freezer, we use zip-sealing plastic bags. We try squeezing the air out of the bags or displacing it with a bit of CO_2 from our tank before placing the bags in the freezer. This is not an ideal way to store hops, but for the few weeks that a bag lasts us, the method works acceptably well. Ideally, hops should be stored in oxygen barrier bags with the air displaced by a gas such as nitrogen. However, this is beyond the realm of the hobbyist.

*There's nothing like a **plastic Rubbermaid bin** with a snap-on lid for storing grain. Tupperware bowls are good, too.*

– 4 –

GRAIN MILLS

ALTHOUGH ANY BREWER WHO HAS ADVANCED beyond simple can kits may be interested in milling grain, it is usually the veteran all-grain brewers who think about grain mills. They avoid buying pre-crushed grain and pre-packaged grains. Instead, serious all-grain brewers typically buy malt in 50-pound sacks in order to realize substantial cost savings (they usually use 8 to 10 pounds of grain per 5-gallon batch) and to capture the freshness of newly milled grain.

If you want to join the ranks of serious all-grain brewers, you will have two somewhat contradictory goals: (1) you will want to crush the starchy endosperm (the inside of the barley grain) into a fairly fine powder that is removed from the husks so that it's exposed to the brewing water during the mash; and (2) you will want the husks to remain relatively intact so they form a good filter bed when you sparge the grains.

Most homebrewers use commercially available mills for crushing grains, although a number have even built their own.

ALTERNATIVES TO MILLING

Do you really need to mill? For most novice homebrewers, the answer is "no." A mill can cost as much as an entire basic brewing kit, and because you're only using a pound or so of grain for color and added body, it's more cost-effective to buy the grain pre-crushed at a homebrew supply shop. But what if you want to brew that tasty recipe you saw for an extract-based stout that called for a bit of black patent malt, and the shop did not have any pre-crushed? Well, there are a few simple alternatives that will get you by in a pinch:

- ✔ Rolling pin
- ✔ Coffee grinder
- ✔ Food processor

The easiest way to crush grains with a rolling pin is to put the grains in a zip-sealing bag and then crush them. This is not easy, (1) because the grains likely will be harder than you expect, therefore will not crush easily; and (2) because the rolling pin tends to push the grains away rather than crushing them. As a result, it's very difficult to end up with anything approaching a consistent crush. We've occasionally resorted to bashing the grain with a mallet. Even though this gives us a certain barbaric pleasure, it, too, produces less than optimal results. Usually we end up with more whole, uncracked kernels than we'd like. Because we're using only small amounts of grain and we're not relying on it for much (if any) of the body, we either don't worry about it or we add a little extra grain to compensate for the relatively poor results.

Manufacturers of small, hand-held coffee grinders (such as that shown on page 48) often advertise that they are capable of crushing grains — and they are, they just don't do it very well. This grinder produced a very uneven crush. Some grains were not touched at all; others were completely pulverized, leaving no

If you're just using a small amount of grain to add color to your brew, a small hand-held **coffee grinder** *might be the best way to grind the grain.*

traces of intact husk. This would be completely unacceptable for an all-grain batch; but again, if you're using only small amounts of grain to achieve the color, you can probably get away with it. By the way, this grinder did quite well grinding coffee.

The third option is a food processor, which requires a grinding attachment to handle grains. Kitchen Aid sells such an attachment, but it costs as much as some of the better malt mills (described in the next section). Like the coffee grinder, the food processor delivers an uneven crush; so, given the cost of purchasing the grinding attachment, we cannot recommend this approach. However, if you've already got the food processor and its attachment, you will probably find that it produces slow runoff times and low extraction rates. Our test crush had far more flour than we wanted and few intact husks. Some homebrewers report that the Kitchen Aid grinding attachment works well for them. So if you already have one, give it a try, but we don't recommend buying one for brewing purposes.

Although none of these approaches produce exceptional results, you can partially compensate for the poor husk integrity by using a grain bag. If you've got other ideas, give them a try.

Homebrewers are an inventive lot, and many people have undoubtedly found other ways to crush grain. ("Hey, Bob! Think I could just back my pickup truck over that sack a few dozen times?") But let's move on to ways of doing it right.

COMMERCIALLY AVAILABLE MILLS

There are two general categories of grain mills used by homebrewers: grinders and roller mills. Grinders tend to cut the kernels of the grain, whereas roller mills burst the husk by crushing it. Generally, all roller mills maintain better husk integrity and offer improved yields than do the grinders.

The Corona Mill

The Corona Mill, a simple grinder made in South America, has been used by homebrewers for many years and is available at most homebrew supply shops. Although it is made for crushing corn,

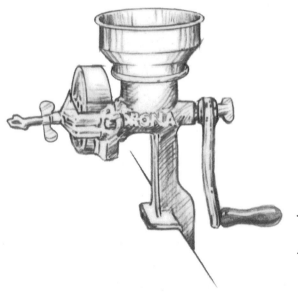

*The **Corona Mill** is manufactured for crushing corn, but it does a good job of crushing malt in limited amounts.*

it does fairly well for limited amounts of malt. The most attractive feature of the Corona is its price — it can still be purchased for less than $50 (as of early 1995).

Although all-grain brewers do not regard the Corona Mill as capable of delivering a high-quality crush (it is prone to delivering slow-runoff mashes and it is difficult to adjust), quite a few continue to use it. It's a worthwhile choice for the brewer whose equipment budget is limited, and it certainly gets you into the all-grain game. However, we recommend that you spend a few dollars more and move up to any roller mill.

Roller Mills

Several excellent roller mills came on the market in the early 1990s, and now advanced homebrewers can produce a high-quality crush, one in which the husk is structurally intact — not shredded or ground into flour — and the starchy endosperm is both crushed and exposed. Roller mills that are commercially available today include:

✔ JSP MaltMill
✔ Listermann PhilMill
✔ Glatt Mill
✔ Valley Mill
✔ BrewTek Malt Mill

When you start looking for a new mill, there are several things to consider:

✔ Quality of crush (sieve test, adjustability)
✔ Roller construction (material, knurling pattern, diameter, and length)
✔ Usability (cranking torque, throughput, hopper size)
✔ Craftsmanship
✔ Warranty
✔ Price
✔ Ability to be motorized

Generally, all roller mills should deliver a good crush, and crush tests have shown that indeed all of the roller mills on the market today do so. The tests involved running grain samples through each of the mills and then analyzing the amount of material that passed through or was retained by screens with varying sieve sizes. The tests also showed that better crush results can be achieved (more material separated from husks) by running the grain through the mill a second time. Regarding the quality of crush for these mills, the Corona tends to shear husks and produce a poor crush, but all the roller mills produce acceptable crushes.

If you are interested in more information on crush quality, in 1994, *Zymurgy* magazine published a detailed article by Bob Gorman, Steve Stroud, and Mike Fertsch that compared several of these mills.

When you look at the rollers, there are several things to keep in mind:

- ✔ Longer rollers deliver better throughput
- ✔ Larger-diameter rollers crush more easily
- ✔ Surface texture is important on small rollers but less so on large rollers

Most rollers used in these mills are made of cold-rolled steel. However, stainless-steel rollers are also available for the JSP MaltMill.

Most roller mills on the market today have some sort of knurled pattern on the roller to provide friction and help pull the grains down into the crushing mechanism. Whereas large rollers tend to pull the grain through naturally, small-diameter rollers need some sort of friction to help pull the grain down into the gap to crush it. So, given the relatively small diameter of mills used by homebrewers, the knurl, or pattern on the roller, is important. Knurled patterns can be either long grooves that travel the length of the roller or, more commonly, a rough diamond shape.

Adjustability of the rollers is important to some homebrewers. By tightening the roller gap, they can produce a grist that is close to flour, which is desirable with some grains. But for the most part you will probably keep your mill at a constant setting, and a nonadjustable mill will provide good results. If you are looking for adjustability, it is best to have the rollers adjust in parallel. That way you get a consistent crush across the entire length of the roller.

The usability of a certain mill is something you'll want to gauge for yourself. Ideally, try to find a shop that stocks several mills and try them out. The following are some of the things that affect usability:

The force required to turn the handle. This is important if you're not planning to motorize your mill. You want a mill that turns easily when the hopper is filled.

Throughput. This is the amount of grain that you can crush in a given time (essentially the speed at which the mill operates). Some homebrewers are willing to sacrifice throughput to save money because the time it takes to crush 8 to 10 pounds of grain is not significant to most hobbyists. To others, throughput is very important, especially those working with 15-gallon batches.

Hopper size. This is an issue because ideally you should not have to stop every few minutes to refill the hopper. If you're motorizing the mill, (1) you may be able to simply feed the hopper continuously, in which case this isn't a problem, or (2) you may be able to build an extension to your hopper.

Ease of use. Included here are how the crank feels in your hand, whether the crank is oriented in a way that feels natural to you, how the crushed grain comes out, where the collection bucket is placed, and so on. These are issues that you need to judge for yourself.

Craftsmanship. There are several things to consider when you judge the craftsmanship of a mill. Look for signs of solid construction, that is, good-quality materials, smooth surfaces, tight fit of parts, and so on. If the mill has plastic or wooden components, will they withstand the rigors of your home brewery?

Let's take a detailed look at the five malt mills we listed earlier and see how they work and what features they incorporate.

The JSP MaltMill

This was among the first of the roller mills available to homebrewers. The mill uses two 1½-inch diameter by 10-inch long rollers with a diamond-knurl pattern. A crank drives one roller, while the other roller is turned by friction as grain moves through the gap. The hopper and base are constructed of fiber board, and the unit is built to sit on top of a bucket, which catches the crushed grain. This mill is easy to crank and delivers the fastest throughput of any of the mills on the market today. It is available in either an adjustable or fixed-gap model, and it can be motorized easily. Brewers who have used the fixed-gap model report that they get good crushes with all types of grain and appreciate the savings they gain by skipping a feature they don't need.

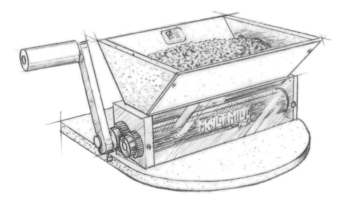

The JSP MaltMill, one of the first roller mills available to home-brewers, delivers the fastest throughput of any of the mills on the market today.

The JSP MaltMill is backed by a lifetime guarantee, the best guarantee of all the mills. The street price of the JSP MaltMill ranges from $99 to $109 for the fixed-gap model and rises to about $125 for the adjustable model. It is available from Jack Schmidling Productions, although many homebrew supply shops stock the mill or can get it.

The Listermann PhilMill

The Listermann PhilMill is a single-roller mill that grinds grain against a fixed metal plate. The plate is actually slightly curved, leaving the grain in contact with the roller as it moves downward, giving it a better crush. The quality of the crush can be adjusted by turning a screw that pushes or releases the metal plate, although we found both the crush and the screw fairly hard to adjust consistently. The roller is about 2½ inches long and 1½ inches in diameter, with a diamond-knurl pattern. The

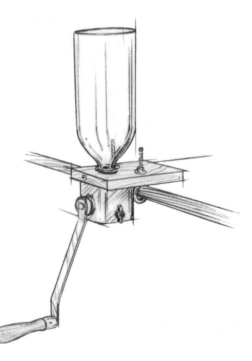

The PhilMill is a single-roller mill that grinds grain against a fixed metal plate.

base is oak and is fairly compact — it attaches to a counter or table top with two hooks and wing nuts. The hopper, which is not included, is simply a 2-liter soda bottle whose mouth fits into a hole above the roller. This bottle will hold about 2 pounds of uncrushed malt. The unit cranks fairly easily, but throughput is about half that of the JSP MaltMill. The unit is sturdy and well built, but we saw no mention of a guarantee in the package. Instructions are provided for motorizing the mill using a drill. The PhilMill retails for about $70. It is available from Listermann Manufacturing.

The Glatt Mill

The Glatt Mill is a two-roller mill that uses plastic gears to drive both rollers. The unit comes with a fair-sized stainless-steel hopper that will hold about 2 pounds, and it cranks fairly easily. The rollers are small — about 1½ inches by 4 inches.

Like the PhilMill, this mill has about half the throughput of the JSP MaltMill. We've heard some reports of problems with the plastic gears, but the plastic is a carbon-impregnated nylon that

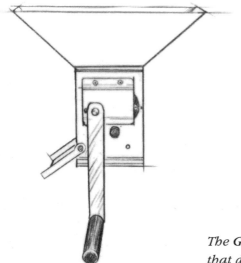

*The **Glatt Mill** has plastic gears that drive two small rollers.*

should be durable for most malt milling applications. We suspect that the problems were only in earlier models. This unit retails for about $115. It's sturdy and the most visually attractive of the mills sold today. The Glatt is a good mill. Unfortunately, Glatt may be out of business as of late 1995; but given the durability of their mills, you will most likely continue to see them in use by homebrewers for some time.

The Valley Mill

The Valley Mill is very similar to the JSP MaltMill. It uses long rollers (9 inches by 1 inch in diameter), one of which crank-drives directly. The other is driven by friction. Grain is fed through the top from a very large, tall hopper. (Hoppers on the Glatt and JSP mills are more flared.) The instructions claim the hopper will hold 4 pounds — it's certainly one of the largest hoppers we've seen. One nice thing about this mill is that the

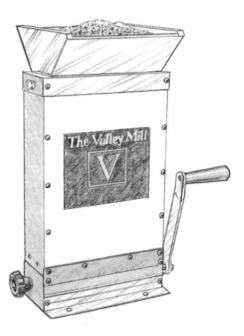

The Valley Mill has two long rollers: one crank-drives directly, and the other drives by friction.

rollers adjust in parallel via a spring-loaded cam mechanism with several preset stops. The JSP mill, by comparison, adjusts at only one end. The Valley Mill should theoretically deliver a more consistent crush. The mill can be motorized by attaching an electric drill. However, you will need to build your own base for the mill. This can be as simple as cutting a rectangle in a piece of wood and setting it on a bucket. When comparing costs of mills, consider what it will cost to buy or build the base. The Valley Mill sells for $99 in the United States and $145 in Canada. It is available from Valley Brewing Equipment.

The BrewTek Mill

The BrewTek Mill from Brewer's Resource came on the market in mid-1995. It uses two stainless-steel rollers that are about 2 inches in diameter by 2 inches long. A hand crank directly drives one roller; the second roller is turned by friction. Both rollers are knurled and adjust in parallel. The wooden base has

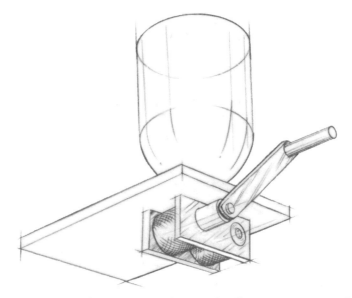

*The **BrewTek Mill** has two stainless-steel rollers: one operates by hand crank, the other by friction.*

a hole drilled above the rollers into which a soda bottle fits to serve as the hopper (similar to the PhilMill). A 2-liter soda bottle should give you a hopper capacity of about 2 pounds. The larger-diameter roller crushes well, but its short length allows throughput that's just slightly better than the PhilMill and the Glatt but consistently less than the JSP or Valley Mill. The BrewTek Mill retails for about $90. It is available from Brewer's Resource.

Which one do we recommend? All these mills are fine products and are priced competitively, given their quality and performance. We like the simplicity and low price of the PhilMill, but the JSP MaltMill has the best throughput and the best guarantee. We don't like its adjustment mechanism, however; so if adjustability is not critical to you, the nonadjustable JSP MaltMill would be a good selection. We do like the adjustment mechanism of the Valley Mill and its large hopper, and we like the fat rollers on the BrewTek Mill. The choice is yours, of course, and you could even try building your own mill.

BUILDING A WOODEN ROLLER MILL

If you're a woodworker or at least a wood tinkerer, then you can build a simple wooden roller mill. It is definitely not what you want for all-grain brewing. This mill is suited for extract brewers who like to add a pound or two of adjuncts and want something better than a rolling pin to crush their grains. The main problem will be obtaining something suitable for rollers. If you have access to a lathe, then you're in good shape. Otherwise you might have to visit a wood shop, in which case you may pay more for the roller than it's worth. You need to locate a piece of close-grained hardwood, such as hard maple, hickory, or walnut, that is at least 16 inches long and 1½ inches to 2 inches in diameter. Old-style rolling pins might work if you can find them. The wood you choose must be straight; if it is warped, it cannot be used. One clever homebrewer used a broken baseball bat, which should do nicely as long as it meets the minimum criteria stated above. You can work around the taper.

If you've managed to locate a suitable piece of hardwood — and you don't need a lathe — then skip to the next section. If you do have to turn your roller, read on.

Lathes can differ, so mount the wood stock on your lathe according to the instructions for turning a long piece of wood. Turn the entire length to a uniform diameter. The final diameter should match a standard wood drill-bit dimension. (You will be running the roller through holes, so choose a diameter based on standard drill-bit sizes.) Leave the wood in the lathe to cut the grooves. It's easier this way: You can use the tool rest as a guide, and the wood is safely clamped in place, but you must figure out some way to lock the lathe to keep it from turning. Once the grooves are cut, you can turn down a 3-inch length on each end to allow for handles — it's your choice.

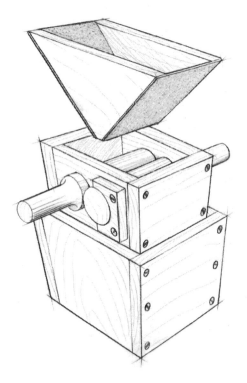

If you're an extract brewer who likes to add a pound or two of malt to your brew — and if you like to work with wood — you can build this wooden roller mill. The frame can be either of plywood or dimensional lumber; the rollers must be hardwood (old rolling pins are excellent). The roller mill frame, which is also the collection box, is made of ½-in. plywood.

Directions for Cutting Grooves

1. Mark a line 4 inches in from each end.
2. Clamp the wood into a vise or secure it somehow to your bench top. (Skip if it's still in the lathe).
3. With the corner of a very sharp chisel, cut 1/16"-deep grooves lengthwise between the two lines. Make the cuts every 1/4" until you've completely covered the roller. It does not have to be precise. You're just giving a "bite" to the rollers so they will be able to grab the grain.
4. Saw the roller into two equal-sized rollers.

Frame

The roller frame can be made of either plywood or dimensional lumber. If you want it to last, use a hardwood such as oak or maple. Whatever wood you choose must be clear of knots and warps. While we're on the subject, if you choose dimensional lumber, use 1 inch by 4 inch material and don't worry that it's not exactly 4 inches wide. That fact has been taken into consideration.

Building a Roller Frame

1. Cut two pieces 6" long x 4" wide and two end pieces 4" x 4".
2. Locate and mark a center line lengthwise on the 6" side pieces.
3. Locate the exact center of this line on both side pieces.
4. Divide the diameter of the rollers by 2, measure this distance on either side of the center line, and mark these points on both side pieces.
5. Drill a hole the same diameter as the rollers at these points for both side pieces.
6. Cut another piece of wood 3" long x 4" wide. This piece will adjust the gap between the rollers.

7. At the exact center of this piece, drill another hole the same diameter as the rollers.

8. Cut this piece into two pieces along the 4" dimension to get two pieces that are 2" x 3".

9. Using eight #6 x 2" screws, assemble the frame. See illustration of wooden roller mill on page 59.

10. Place the gap adjustment pieces as shown, leaving at most a ¹⁄₁₆" gap between the rollers. (Use a drum sander to enlarge the holes if necessary.)

11. Secure the gap adjustors with screws.

Collection Box

The base is also the collection box, and the roller mill frame sits down inside it. It is made of ½-inch plywood.

Directions

1. Cut the two sides, 7⁹⁄₁₆" long x 6" high.

2. Cut the two end pieces, 7¹⁄₁₆" long x 6" high.

3. Cut the bottom, 7⁹⁄₁₆" long x 6¹⁄₁₆" wide.

4. Assemble all sides to the bottom with glue and twelve #6 x 1½" screws. See illustration on page 59.

5. Cut out two 2½" x ½" wood strips that are 5" to 6" long, and two others that are 6" to 7" long. (These can be made out of any scrap wood you have.)

6. Glue and clamp the strips on the inside of the collection box, ½" below the top edge of the sides.

Hopper Construction

Now all you need is a hopper to feed grain into the rollers. Using ½-inch plywood and ⅛-inch masonite, you can build a suitable hopper.

Constructing a Hopper

1. Cut two end pieces out of ½" plywood, 6¾" wide x 3⅛" high. The sides of the end pieces are trimmed at a 45-degree angle, leaving about a ½"-wide bottom.
2. Cut the two masonite sides 3½" wide x 3⅛" high.
3. Attach the masonite sides to the end pieces with eight 1"-long #6 wood screws.
4. Attach the hopper assembly to the frame by setting the narrow end of the hopper into the frame and securing it so that the bottom of the hopper is about 1 inch below the top edge of the frame with two 1¼"-long #6 wood screws (see illustration).

Hopper Construction

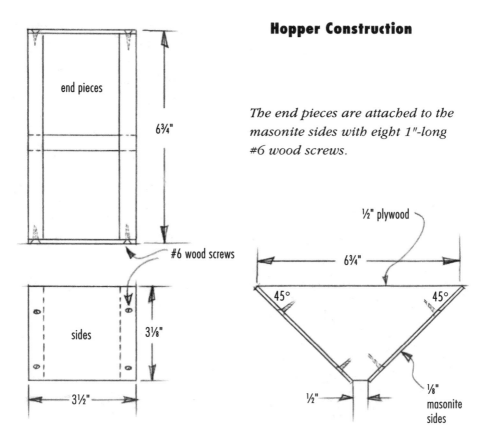

The end pieces are attached to the masonite sides with eight 1"-long #6 wood screws.

To use, set the hopper and frame assembly inside the collection box and fill the hopper with grain. Grasp a roller in each hand and turn them toward one another, pulling the grain down between the rollers. It may take some effort. Jams can be cleared by reversing the turning direction. Just don't turn the roller too far, or whole grains will drop down into the collection box.

If you are serious about all-grain brewing, you might consider building a motorized roller mill (see illustration). Chris Barnhart of Geneseo, Illinois, built a compact, motorized roller mill that delivers excellent crushes comparable in quality to those delivered by JSP MaltMill. Milling the grain on brew day is as simple as turning on the mill and filling the hopper. For Chris Barnhart's full instructions, see Appendix A, "Building a Motorized Mill."

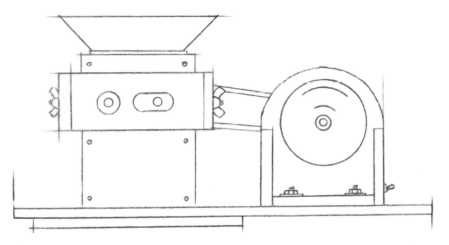

Mill and motor are mounted on a particle board base that is cut to fit over a drywall bucket.

–5–

MASHING, LAUTERING, AND SPARGING

WHAT PROPERTIES ARE WE LOOKING FOR in a mashing vessel? Well, obviously it has to hold hot liquid — anything that leaks or melts at high temperatures would be a poor choice. We would like our mashing vessel to be insulated so that it holds heat. If not insulated, it should be able to withstand the application of direct heat, so it can be placed on a stove or burner to maintain an appropriate mash temperature. Beyond that, anything goes.

Several years ago some of the homebrewing literature recommended approaches that required mashing in one container and then moving the grain to a separate container for sparging (rinsing the grain with hot water). For most brewers, any approach that requires moving the mash from one vessel to another will be a poor choice. It's much easier to have one vessel that serves for both mashing and lautering (straining the sweet wort off the spent grains after mashing).

As with all homebrewing equipment, the mashing vessel needs to meet the requirements of the individual homebrewer. Whereas we do not recommend approaches that require moving the mash from vessel to vessel, that approach does work well for some brewers using a step mash.

When we talk about sparging the grains, we should be aware of how liquids flow through a grain bed so that we get as much of the sugars from the grain as we can. In a mashing vessel, fluids flow through the grain bed following the path of least resistance. The water tends to flow along certain paths rather than uniformly flowing through the grain. This forms the equivalent of rivers through the grain bed and is often referred to as "channeling." There are various solutions to this problem, including using blades to cut the mash bed and using an outlet system (manifold) that draws from many points to minimize the chance of a single strong channel forming. The false bottom is probably the best method for reducing channeling, although other methods, such as the manifold, do quite well. Again, this is of mostly academic interest to homebrewers, and the most intense homebrewers can spend hours discussing it over a cool pint of bitter. All the approaches we discuss here will produce good beers on a small scale.

Keep in mind when working with mashing equipment that some heat energy will be lost to the equipment when you add your heated strike water. This is less important when using a mashing method that allows you to apply direct heat to the mashing vessel, but brewers using picnic coolers and similar vessels should try to minimize the heat loss. You can do this by pre-heating your mashing vessel; fill it with 180°F water. The temperature isn't especially critical, but very hot water could warp the liner of your picnic cooler. Let the water sit for a few minutes, and then empty it just as you're ready to start your mash.

Some heat energy is invariably lost during the mash. This heat loss can be minimized by insulating your mashing vessel. Some brewers simply toss a blanket or sleeping bag over the vessel; however, a more elegant approach is to fit an insulation layer around the vessel. Cutting to fit something like the space blankets sold at outdoor stores works well.

Approaches to Mash-Tun Construction

The mash tun is one area in which homebrewers have a wide latitude for good, solid, workable, home-built solutions. Some of the approaches most widely used include:

✔ Using an oblong picnic cooler
✔ Building a mash tun from a round, cylindrical water cooler
✔ Modifying a beer keg

Mashing in a Picnic Cooler

Large chest-style picnic coolers make ideal mash tuns because they are well insulated and inexpensive. For a 5-gallon setup, look for a 34-quart cooler (about $10 to $15). The next size up is usually the 48-quart cooler, which will handle 10- or 15-gallon batches without a problem. Although 48-quart coolers are larger than you'd really want when doing 5-gallon batches (they may give you a shallow grain bed), quite a few homebrewers use that size without a problem. For very large batches, 60- or 80-quart coolers are reasonable. One consideration when choosing a cooler is its resistance to heat. If you can find a brand that claims to withstand 170°F temperatures, you're ahead of the game. If not, you're still okay. Most of them don't warp too badly, and even if they do, they'll still hold heat well enough to mash — and besides, they're cheap. Building a new one every year or so is no big deal.

Once you have the cooler, you may need to drill out a drainage plug if it doesn't already have one. Because we're using ½-inch-diameter CPVC pipe for this project, drill a ⅝-inch-diameter hole (the outer diameter of a ½-inch-diameter CPVC pipe).

Although the drainage hole in a cooler is usually on the side, having the hole in the bottom is actually a bit more workable in many situations. Next, you'll have to build a drainage manifold to lay in the bottom of the cooler.

Materials for Mash-Tun Construction

6' of ½"-diameter CPVC pipe
Four 90-degree elbows for ½"-diameter CPVC pipe
Five tee connectors for ½"-diameter CPVC pipe
Food-grade silicone or epoxy sealant
½"-diameter I.D. (inside diameter) poly tube
Picnic cooler

Tools

Hack saw
⅝"-diameter drill bit and drill (if the cooler does not have a drain)

Directions

1. Measure the length of the cooler bed. Subtract 4" and cut four lengths of CPVC tubing to that length.
2. Measure the width. Subtract 4" and divide by 3. Cut six lengths of CPVC tubing to that length. Cut one of these lengths in half. Now use a hacksaw and cut thin slots in all the pipes, about one-third of the way through. Assemble the manifold as shown in the illustration on page 68.
3. You can glue the manifold together, but it will be easier to clean if you make it easy to disassemble. One idea that works well is to permanently glue the two end-units together, and then just piece together the four long rods when it's time to brew.

You could add a valve to the manifold outlet if you wish, but a simple and less expensive approach is to use a length of vinyl hose, a hose clamp, and a pinchcock type (siphon) clamp. Push a length of hose over the outlet tube and secure it with the hose clamp. Feed the hose through the siphon clamp. This will be your valve. By closing and opening this clamp, you can adjust the flow of your runoff. If you wish to use a valve, CPVC ball valves are available for about $3 to $5. Compression fittings with gaskets are also available for CPVC tubes, and if your cooler does not already have a drain plug in the wall, consider using one of these. Before drilling through the wall, remember you could also go through the bottom rather than the side.

You could use a grain bag in conjunction with the manifold if you really want to, but we've had no problems with the manifold by itself, so save the money from the grain bags for better ingredients. In Greg Noonan's book *Brewing Lager Beer,* he suggests that if you're using a manifold like this, build in a flush tube so you can recover stuck sparges and so on. Stuck sparges that refuse to runoff aren't often a problem, and most homebrewers we have met who've built manifolds like this don't

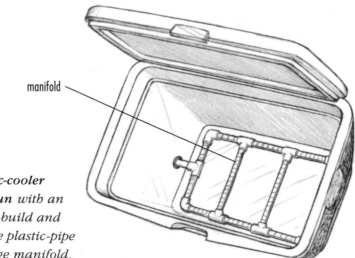

manifold

*A **picnic-cooler** **mash tun** with an easy-to-build and effective plastic-pipe drainage manifold.*

use the flush tubes. One other idea that seems to work well is to replace the CPVC with copper pipe, which is readily available at most plumbing supply stores and is fairly inexpensive and easy to work with.

A couple of approaches will work for introducing sparge water to the picnic-cooler mash tun. A simple hose attached to a boiling kettle will work fine (see the description of the JSP EasySparger on page 83 and 84). You could also construct a simple sparge sprayer out of CPVC pipe. Simply obtain two lengths of thin CPVC supply line (⅜ inch will be fine) and cut one to the length of your cooler. Next, cap one end of this pipe and drill very small holes in the pipe (see illustration below).

To do this, we acquired a couple of ⅟₃₂-inch drill bits from a hobby shop (they break easily!) and drilled holes about ½ inch apart on one side only along the entire length of the pipe. Glue the second length of CPVC, which is cut a bit longer than the cooler's width, to the long tube and at a right angle to it. The second pipe simply supports the sprayer and provides stability when it's positioned over the top of the cooler.

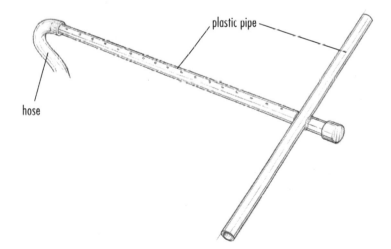

*You can make a **simple sprayer** to fit into a picnic-cooler mash tun out of two pieces of plastic pipe. (This is a bottom view: the holes need to point down to spray onto the grain bed.)*

Now push the vinyl tube over the end of the CPVC tube. Depending on the size of your hose, you may have to add a hose barb adapter to hook the CPVC to the vinyl hose. If you use ½-inch-diameter CPVC pipe, a ⅝-inch-diameter I.D. (inside diameter) poly hose will fit tightly over the end. Then siphon the sparge water into the sprayer.

Mashing in a Water Cooler

The large, round, cylindrical water coolers that you often see on the back of construction trucks make ideal mashing vessels. They are available in sizes that are large enough for home mashing, and they are well insulated. The brand most often used by homebrewers is the Gott cooler, which is made by Rubbermaid.

This cooler is known to withstand the heat of a mash without warping, as often happens with cheaper coolers. The 10-gallon size is the one you'll want; it usually runs about $50 at

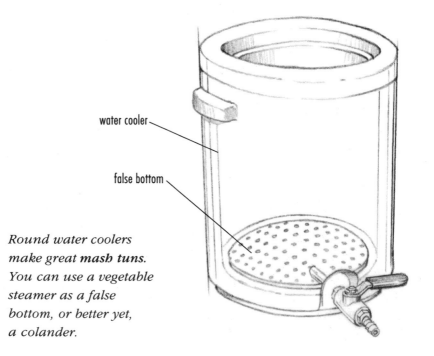

water cooler

false bottom

Round water coolers make great mash tuns. You can use a vegetable steamer as a false bottom, or better yet, a colander.

outdoor or construction supply stores, although it can be found at discount warehouses for as little as $30.

An easy way to use the cooler is to put a vegetable steamer in the bottom of the cooler and then set the grains on that. We've found this works acceptably well, but it does tend to let a lot of grains through. Another idea is to get a colander that's smaller than the circumference of the cooler and set it upside down in the bottom of the cooler. You may want to rig some kind of drainage device, such as the JSP EasyMasher (available from Jack Schmidling Productions), to go inside the colander. Phil's Phalse Bottom (available from Listermann Manufacturing) is an excellent choice for use as a drainage system with the Gott coolers, and this is the method that we recommend. The Phil's Phalse Bottom is simply a heavy plastic cone that's perforated with holes. It's available at many homebrew supply shops.

You can also build a manifold to go in the bottom of the cooler, much like that described in the previous section.

One thing that you'll want to do with the water cooler is to install a valve of some kind. The pushbutton spigot is entirely inadequate (unless you want to hold in the button for the hour or so that a sparge might take).

Modified Keg with False Bottom

Modified kegs, if not the most commonly used mash tun, are probably the most talked about and respected. Kegs are sturdy and inexpensive, and they work well. You can apply heat directly to them, and you can modify them with false bottoms and valves to make sparging simple. They are also easy to clean.

The first thing you will need is a legally obtained keg. Do not think that paying the deposit for a full half-barrel, consuming the contents, and then keeping the keg is a legal means of acquiring one. It is not. Instead you will need to talk to the distributors in your area. Sometimes they are willing to help, and sometimes they'll barely give you the time of day. Other sources are salvage

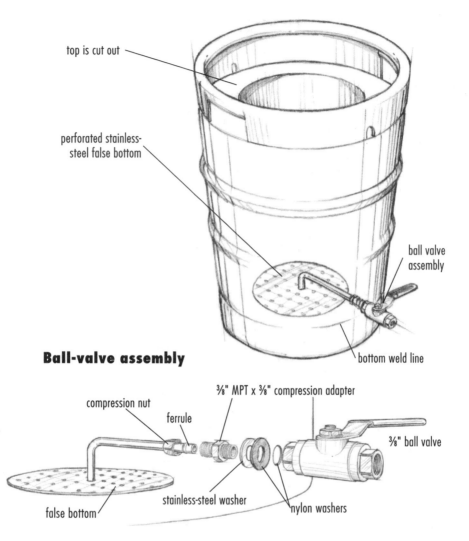

top is cut out

perforated stainless-steel false bottom

ball valve assembly

bottom weld line

Ball-valve assembly

compression nut

ferrule

⅜" MPT x ⅜" compression adapter

⅜" ball valve

false bottom

stainless-steel washer

nylon washers

Kegs with false bottoms are probably the most common form of mash tun, but the actual work that goes into modifying these tough stainless-steel vessels is considerable.

yards and scrap-metal dealers. Just don't be discouraged. If you cannot locate one, SABCO Industries sells a cleaned and fully modified keg for a reasonable price. When you consider the amount of work and tools required to modify a keg, the price is a veritable bargain.

Before you begin to modify your own keg, you will need an assortment of gear:

Tools

Hearing and eye protection. You are about to embark on the noisiest job you've ever started.

Variable-speed sabre saw or reciprocating saw. A two-speed unit is not good enough. The slowest setting is still way too fast.

Five bi-metal saw blades (32 teeth per inch or better). You may need more. A small angle grinder would work fabulously for cutting a keg.

Center punch (or nail and hammer)

⅜" electric drill, variable speed preferred

An assortment of drill bits

Grinding wheel

Materials for Modifying a Keg

⅜" copper tubing

8" diameter perforated stainless steel for false bottom

One ⅜" compression nut and ferrule

Two ⅜" male pipe thread (MPT) x ⅜" compression adapters

One ½" I.D. (inside diameter) stainless-steel washer

Two ½" I.D. (inside diameter) nylon washers

One ⅜" ball valve with ⅜" female pipe thread (FPT)

12" square perforated stainless steel

Permanent marking pen

Lightweight oil

Note: You are working with stainless steel, which is tough stuff. The basic rule when working with it is, the slower, the better. Take your time! A few drops of lightweight oil applied during the drilling and cutting can help extend the life of your tools.

Directions

1. Without a blade in the saw, set the sabre saw against the inside top of the keg. You are finding out how close you can cut to the handles, as the saw body will be the limiting factor.
2. Mark a point where the blade will be cutting. Draw a circle around the top inside of this mark. In our case, we were able to make an opening 12" in diameter in our keg.
3. With a center punch (or nail and hammer), mark a point ⅛" from the line inside this circle.
4. Drill a ¼" hole at that point. (It is easier if you drill a smaller hole first and then enlarge it).
5. Install a blade in the saw, oil it, and at a slow speed carefully cut the top out of the keg. Plan on spending at least 45 minutes on this phase.
6. With the grinding wheel in the drill, grind off all sharp edges.
7. Mark a point ⅜" above the bottom weld line.
8. Drill a ½"-diameter hole. (Again, start small, then enlarge the hole.)

Note: You are done cutting and about to start assembling your mashing vessel. This is a good time to scrub the interior of the keg. It will save time later. Also clean all parts before final assembly. That too will help.

9. Place the stainless-steel washer and then a nylon washer on the pipe-thread end (the large end) of a ⅜" MPT x ⅜" compression adapter.
10. Insert this into the ½"-diameter hole. It will fit tightly, and you will have to use a wrench to finish the job. You may have to enlarge the hole slightly beyond ½".
11. Place the other nylon washer over the pipe threads.
12. Wrap Teflon tape around the threads.
13. Thread on a ⅜" ball valve and tighten. Be sure to use a wrench on the inside to hold the adapter in place.

14. Drill a ⅜"-diameter hole in the center of the perforated metal (false bottom).
15. Bend the end of the ⅜"-diameter copper tubing to 90 degrees. This bent end goes through the false bottom.
16. Set the false bottom and tube assembly in the bottom of the keg.
17. Measure and cut the copper tubing so that it fits into the inside ⅜" compression fitting.
18. Attach the tubing to the ⅜" compression fitting with a compression nut and ferrule.
19. Add a ⅜" MPT × ⅜" compression fitting to the ball valve output. By using a ⅜" compression nut, you can either connect this to your counterflow chiller or add a small piece of ⅜" copper tubing for a spigot and attach a vinyl hose.

Note: Instead of using the adapters, washers, and all, you could just take the keg and have two ⅜" female nipples welded to the hole. A welded nipple will also be easier to clean and sanitize. You would need a ⅜" male nipple to attach the ball valve and a ⅜" MPT to ⅜" compression adapter to attach the copper tube. Wrap the male threads with Teflon tape before installing.

You're done. But before you start brewing beer for the first time, fill the keg with 12 gallons of water and add a gallon of vinegar. Bring the mixture to a full boil and boil it for about 15 minutes. Drain. Now everything should be ready for your first batch in your new mash tun.

Although modifying a keg is not outside the capabilities of many homebrewers, it is a dirty, noisy job, and it can often be done with cleaner, more aesthetically pleasing results by someone who has done it before or by someone with a plasma cutter, who could do it in a minute. Several companies will sell you modified kegs for use as mashing or boiling vessels, and most will even sell you a complete turnkey brewery system built around modified beer kegs. Pico-Brewing Systems has several brewing systems available at reasonable prices. Pico-Brewing also sells a larger setup based on 55-gallon drums, and a smaller setup based on 5-gallon stainless-steel pots. SABCO Industries sells modified beer kegs for use as either mashing or boiling vessels.

One of the better values among complete keg-based mashing systems is the PBS 3K system sold by East Coast Brewing Supply. They also offer systems based on stainless-steel kettles in sizes ranging from 5 to 25 gallons.

COMMERCIALLY AVAILABLE MASH TUNS

Here are three systems that range from easy-to-use to gadget-heads-only.

Mashing in a Brewpot: The EasyMasher Approach

The EasyMasher from Jack Schmidling Productions is an eminently simple system. You take a 32-quart enamel canning pot, drill a hole in the side, and attach a spigot to the outside and a tubular stainless-steel screen to the inside. That's basically it. The mash is held at a constant temperature in the pot either by directly heating it with a stove burner or by calculating your strike water temperature correctly. You can cover the vessel with a large blanket, set it in a pre-warmed (but turned off) oven, or simply let it sit. The volume of mash should, at room temperature, retain heat long enough to reach full conversion. When starch conversion is finished, you sparge in the same pot.

Some homebrewers believe this approach does not rinse the grains thoroughly during the sparge because the wort is pulled from a single point toward the middle of the pot. The manufacturer claims that simply stirring the mash will take care of that problem, but in some test batches with this equipment we found that not stirring at all still gave us respectable yields of 28 points per pound per gallon. When we did stir, we had to recirculate the first runnings again. In sum, the system works well for most homebrewers, is simple, and is inexpensive.

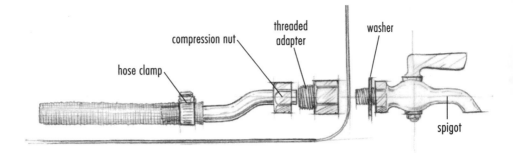

The EasyMasher, which lives up to its name, is basically a tubular stainless-steel screen, a few inches of copper tubing, and a spigot. The screen and tubing is placed inside the vessel and attached, through a hole in the side of the vessel, to the spigot on the outside.

The EasyMasher consists of a 6-inch tube of stainless-steel screen, sealed at the end, and clamped to a 6-inch piece of ⅜-inch-diameter copper tube that's bent in order to let the screen rest on the kettle's bottom. A brass spigot with a lever valve attaches to the outside of the pot and is joined to the copper tube with a compression fitting. (The illustration shows how this fits together.) Although the parts can be obtained at most hardware stores, you can buy the assembly from Jack Schmidling Productions, or you can buy it already installed in a canning pot. The EasyMasher is also available in a size and configuration suitable for modified kegs.

Plastic Buckets with Heating Elements

The BruHeat from BrewCo of Boone, North Carolina, is a plastic bucket with an electric immersion heating element that heats and maintains mash temperature. The buckets are sometimes used in conjunction with a grain bag and a siphon tap in the side of the bucket, although many users seem to prefer having a second vessel for lautering.

The bucket can also double as a brewpot, with the electric elements heating the wort to boiling temperatures. Some

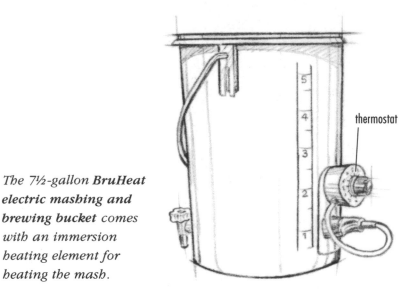

*The 7½-gallon **BruHeat** electric mashing and brewing bucket comes with an immersion heating element for heating the mash.*

thermostat

homebrewers have found that maintaining a vigorous boil with the electric elements is difficult.

The BruHeat has a capacity of 7½ gallons and a 2,750-watt electric heating element. BrewCo warrants the product for one year. This requires a 220-volt power cable, which you must attach yourself (not a big deal if you've ever hooked up a range or clothes dryer, but you must be careful about doing it properly). If your house has a gas stove and dryer, you probably don't have a 220-volt outlet, so this may not be a workable option for you.

The RIMS

The recirculating infusion mash system (RIMS), conceived by Rodney Morris, differs from other mashing methods in that throughout the mashing process, liquid is drained from the bottom of the mashing vessel and pumped back to the top, effectively creating a continuous lautering cycle throughout the mash. In most uses of the RIMS, an in-line heating element maintains mash temperature throughout the process. A thermostatic controller is set up to monitor the mash temperature and reduce current to the element as needed, giving precise control over the mashing environment.

The recirculating infusion mash system offers several attractive benefits, including efficient extraction rates and clear runoff. However, the RIMS involves complicated equipment in most uses and is quite expensive. The hot wort could also be subject to aeration if the system is not set up correctly (although the importance of aeration at this stage is disputed). Many brewers do not want to clarify their wort to such an extent that the cloudy matter that contains material useful for yeast nutrition would be lost.

It's often repeated in homebrewing circles that the electronic controller is the heart of the RIMS, but this is false. It's likely the most talked-about aspect of RIMS, but the heart of the system is really the pump. You could make an inexpensive and uncomplicated recirculating infusion mash system by using a pump in conjunction with a kettle built with a false bottom and ball valve, and controlling the heat with the stove top using an ordinary dial thermometer and the time-tested method of turning the burner on and off. This will not give you the precise temperature control that is one of the attractive benefits of a full RIMS as described by Morris, but it will give you clear running wort. One other inexpensive alternative is to put an appropriately rated dimmer switch on the heater element.

When adapting equipment for use as a RIMS setup, keep in mind that you'll need a pump that is both safe for food and beverage applications and that can handle high temperatures. You'll also want to make sure that your liquid return outlet has some sort of shield, baffle, or other control to keep the liquid from splashing violently into the mash, disturbing the set grain bed. (Doing this will also reduce the aeration risk mentioned above.) If you're developing your own RIMS design, be sure to use ground fault circuit interrupt (GFCI) protection and avoid closing off any tube containing an in-line heating element — you do not want pressure to build up in the line.

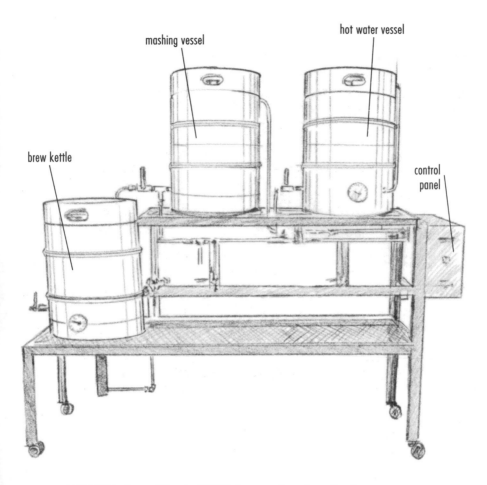

mashing vessel

hot water vessel

brew kettle

control panel

*SABCO's **Brew-Magic RIMS** is a gadget-head's dream.*

Most recirculating infusion mash systems are built around a half-barrel keg mash tun. Commercially, SABCO Industries has a large-scale RIMS built from modified kegs. Theirs is a complete turnkey brewing system that's sold under the name Brew-Magic. It's an attractive system that can produce good beers and offers the best approach to ensuring repeatability and control, but at about $3,000 it's beyond the budget of casual hobbyists.

Less expensive commercial options are in the works. One system developed by Larry Koch of Koch's Koncepts is a RIMS built on a picnic cooler with a pump and in-line heating element for around $300 to $350. The pump and heater are controlled manually, avoiding the need for expensive controllers. A drain below a false bottom feeds the pump, which passes the liquid through the heater and back to the top of the mash bed. The entire unit is compact and folds into the cooler for easy storage.

Some implementations of the RIMS concept have delivered beers with various problems, including thin bodies and grainy tastes. There are, however, many homebrewers in the community producing excellent beers with RIMS. But since most RIMS setups are complicated and expensive, we feel that they don't provide enough benefit to be worth the trouble.

SPARGING AND LAUTERING APPARATUS

The following systems all work well. It's a matter of preference and — of course — money.

Double Bucket Sparger

Probably the best-known approach to sparging is the "Zapap" Lauter Tun described by Charlie Papazian in his book *The New Complete Joy of Homebrewing*. The idea is simple and inexpensive, which is probably why some homebrewers continue using it.

Basically a Zapap consists of two buckets, one inside the other. The inner bucket is drilled with dozens (or hundreds) of small ($\frac{1}{16}$-inch) holes so that the sweet liquor drains from the grain bed into the other bucket. You might want to drill a hole in the bottom bucket for a spigot, although you could just lift the bucket and pour, or siphon off, when you're done.

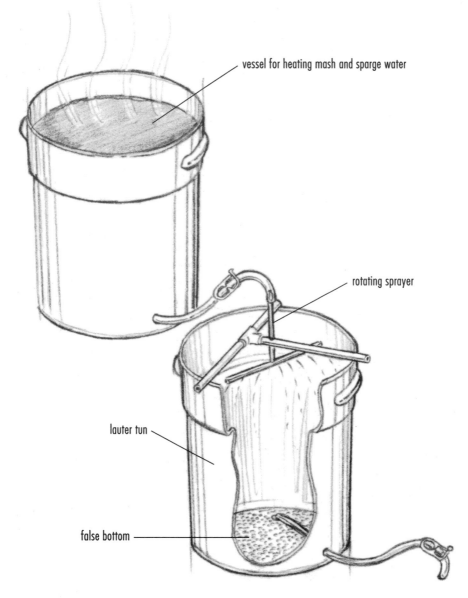

vessel for heating mash and sparge water

rotating sprayer

lauter tun

false bottom

Phil's Lauter Tun, a plastic bucket with a false bottom, comes with a rotating sprayer, similar to a garden hose, that fits through a hole in the lid.

Rotating Sprayers

Phil's Lauter Tun is essentially a plastic bucket with a plastic false bottom and a rotating brass sprayer head suspended through a hole in the lid above the mash bed. A hose attaches to the sprayer to provide the sparge water. As the water feeds through the hose, the sprayer rotates (just like a garden sprinkler), covering the grain bed with hot water. The system — complete with two buckets, the sprayer unit, and Phil's Phalse Bottom — retails for about $40. It is produced by Listermann Manufacturing and is available through many homebrew suppliers (or see Suppliers on page 241). Overall, the system works quite well for sparging, but we prefer avoiding plastic buckets for mashing because they're not insulated and don't hold heat well (again, wrapping the vessel with a blanket or sleeping bag can help minimize heat loss). However, the sprayer itself and the Phalse Bottom are nifty gadgets, and using them in conjunction with a Gott cooler is a good approach that delivers good results at a fairly low cost.

The EasySparger

The JSP EasySparger is an enamel canning pot with two barb connectors. To the upper connector you attach a poly hose from your kitchen faucet. The other connector (lower barb) is for the hot-water exit hose (an HDPE tube), which runs into the mash tun (theoretically the EasyMasher, described on page 76 and 77). The canning pot sits on your stove, and you turn the heat to high. When the water in the pot begins to boil, reduce water flow from the faucet to a steady rate of about 1 gallon per 8 to 10 minutes. Next, raise the water to a level slightly above the grain bed, then open the outlet spigot on the mash tun to match the flow rate of the water from the faucet. The water coming out of the hose will be just above 170°F. We've used the

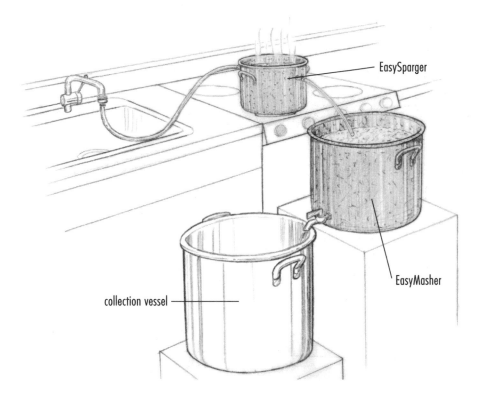

The sink faucet hose is connected to the **EasySparger**, which is connected to the **EasyMasher**. Note the relatively high position of the outlet hose on the EasySparger, which carries hot water to the mash tun. The stainless-steel pot at the bottom of the setup is the **collection vessel**.

EasySparger on several batches and found it to be true to its name — and it delivered good results. It is available from Jack Schmidling Productions.

The Stoelting System

One of the complete mashing systems on the high end of the price scale is the Stoelting Brew System. This is a stainless-steel brewing system built around 7- to 20-gallon vessels. These are not kegs that have been modified. They are custom-fabricated vessels made of type 304 stainless steel with ⅜-inch ball valves and ¼-inch hose nipples. The mash screens are built of tapered bars spaced .03-inch apart. The vessels range in price from $429 to $799, and the mash screens usually run from $179 to $249.

Mash Stirrers

Although some homebrewers are content to let the mash sit throughout the starch-conversion process, others prefer to mix the mash, either periodically or continuously in an effort to maximize their mash efficiency, converting as much starch to sugar as possible. A canoe paddle is the stirrer of choice for many large-scale brewers, and you'll find canoe paddles in quite a few small microbreweries and brewpubs for just that purpose. Kmart and similar discount retailers sell very small canoe paddles (2½ to 3 feet long) that are adequate for many picnic-cooler mash tuns. On page 96, we show how you can cut a simple paddle from a plank. If you make a paddle, avoid using any type of finish on it. If you buy a paddle, you may want to use a light sandpaper to remove the lacquer finish. We do not recommend paddles that are glued together.

Over the years quite a few homebrewers have concocted schemes for putting together motorized mash stirrers. Many of these involve fabricating metal blades shaped like propellers that cut the grain bed as the shaft turns. Motors can be obtained from a variety of sources. One brewer who talked about efficiency at the 1995 AHA conference in Baltimore displayed a mash stirrer powered by a reciprocating saw. In the July/August 1995 issue of *Brewing Techniques,* Sam Johnson described a mashing vessel fitted with a fabricated blade and powered by an ice-cream maker. Johnson's scheme strikes us as an ingenious idea. There is some evidence that stirrers may exacerbate channeling effects.

– 6 –

BREWPOTS AND
THE BOIL

HERE WE DEAL WITH EQUIPMENT used in boiling the wort. Obviously, you need a kettle to hold the wort and a burner for a heat source — and we'll talk about those — but you may also want to consider spoons or other stirrers, lids, and a hopback.

The boil, which should be vigorous and last for at least 60 minutes, serves several functions: It reduces the volume of water in an all-grain wort, thereby increasing the gravity; it extracts the bitterness from hops and changes their character in a process called "isomerization"; it sterilizes the wort, killing any bacteria as well as denaturing any enzymes remaining after the mash; and it drives off unwanted volatile flavor components.

KETTLES: SOME CONSIDERATIONS

Get a big kettle. Bigger than you think you need. If you are doing 5-gallon batches, a 20-quart pot will be too small. You'll want at least a 7-gallon pot (8 gallons would be even better). Keep in mind that in all-grain batches you will be reducing gravity during the boil, so you'll be starting off with about 40 percent more volume than the batch size you want. You also need to add a little extra room to account for vigorous boils that kick off a lot of foam. If you don't have a lot of room, you're going to have a lot of boil-overs and you'll spend a lot of time doing cleanup.

Besides the size of the pot, some other considerations in selecting a good brew kettle include:

Durability. You want a well-made pot that will withstand the rigors of brewing. Ideally it should have sturdy handles because 5 gallons of wort weighs about 45 pounds.

Ease of cleaning. You want a surface that can be cleaned and scrubbed. Sugars and other solids in the wort scorch surfaces, often needing to be scrubbed off. Keep in mind that some materials, such as stainless steel, may react with some of the sanitizers commonly used by homebrewers (e.g., chlorine).

Cost. Trade-offs everywhere. Some of the best pots are the most expensive.

COMMERCIALLY AVAILABLE KETTLES

There are a lot of kettles on the market that you can use for a brewpot. The three most commonly used by homebrewers are:

- ✔ Enamel canning pots
- ✔ Stainless-steel kettles
- ✔ Modified kegs

Enamel canning, or crab, pots work fine for most homebrewers, but the enamel sometimes chips and the pots are not exceptionally durable. If you're planning to be a homebrewer for years to come, a stainless-steel kettle or a modified keg will serve you better and prove more cost-effective over the long run.

Stainless-steel kettles are probably the best choice from a strictly quality perspective. They're built for cooking, are easy to clean, and will last a lifetime if cared for properly; but you should never fill one with a chlorine solution to soak other equipment. Good-quality stainless-steel kettles are available from kitchen and restaurant supply houses. A good source of kettles is Rapids. Expect to pay well over $100 for a good 32-quart kettle.

Brewing kettles in sizes up to 25 gallons are also available from East Coast Brewing Supply. These are good-quality kettles for serious homebrewers, and although they are expensive, they are actually a good value. Expect to pay $100 to $700 for the kettle (depending on size) plus the cost of add-ons, such as sight glasses or thermometers.

If you are into spending a lot of money, Cumberland General Store sells hand-hammered copper pots, which are excellent for beer-making as well as candy-making. Just be prepared for sticker shock. Stainless-steel pots may be pricey, but copper ones can be double that! It's interesting to note, however, that a 40-gallon copper pot doesn't cost much more than a 40-gallon stainless-steel pot. So if you are building a 40-gallon brewery, copper is a viable option. The only problem is that copper pots must be cleaned often, so from this standpoint, stainless steel is easier to live with.

MAKING A BREWPOT FROM A KEG

Modifying a beer keg to use as a brew kettle is a good way to get a stainless-steel vessel that's large enough to accommodate 10-gallon batches. Kegs are durable, easily cleaned, and the perfect size for brewing. The best kegs are the ones with straight sides. The older Hoff-Stevens models that have curved walls and a bunghole in the side are difficult to work with and are a poor choice.

You need to cut the top off the keg and then file down any burrs or rough edges. Instead of cutting the top off from the side of the keg, do it the way most homebrewers (and SABCO Industries) do it: Cut a circular hole in the top, inside the rim, leaving the handles intact. This way you can carry the keg and move it easily. Use a reciprocating saw or sabre saw to cut off the top of the keg, and then use a sanding wheel on a drill to remove the rough burs. For a detailed discussion of modifying a keg, see "Modified Keg with False Bottom" on pages 71 to 76. Again, get your keg legally — don't steal it from a brewery.

You will probably also want to install a ball valve near the bottom of the keg to make it easy to drain. If you put in a valve, you'll want to run a siphon tube from the valve over to the bottom of the pot because the bottom of a keg is domed and a valve in the side is not going to drain all of the liquid. Having a perforated screen at the bottom of the plate helps to remove hops and other matter such as coagulated protein (trub).

Materials for Modifying a Keg to Use as a Brew Kettle

5½-gallon keg with lid cut out
⅜" ball valve with ⅜" FPT
⅜" O.D. (outside diameter) stainless-steel or copper tube
Perforated steel plate
⅜" MPT nipple
⅜" compression nut and ferrule

Welding option

⅜" MPT x ⅜" compression adapter
⅜" FPT coupling
⅜" MPT nipple

Directions for Welding Option

1. First, drill a hole for the coupling in the side of the keg just above the bottom weld.
2. You'll then need to find a welder to weld the coupling to the keg. Omit Washer Option.

Washer option

One ½" I.D. (inside diameter) stainless-steel washer
Two ½" I.D. (inside diameter) nylon washers
⅜" MPT x ⅜" compression adapter

Directions for Washer Option

1. Drill a ½" hole above the bottom weld. Place the stainless-steel washer, followed by a nylon washer, over the pipe threads of the ⅜" MPT x ⅜" compression adapter. Place the adapter inside the keg and through the hole. Place a nylon washer over the pipe threads on the outside of the keg. Wrap Teflon tape around the threads. Thread on the ball valve and tighten.

2. Next cut an 8"-diameter circle from the perforated steel. Drill out the center hole to ⅜". Set the screen in the bottom of the kettle. You'll need to cut the tube to an appropriate length, with one end going through the hole to the bottom of the dome, a 90-degree bend, and then running to the coupling. Attach the tube with the compression nut and ferrule.

COPPER

Because copper serves as a source of yeast nutrients, you might want to keep a small piece of copper around to drop into the brew kettle. A small sawed-off piece of copper tubing will work well.

If you'd like a lid for the kettle, look around for a pizza pan. The larger pans are just about the right size. For each handle, cut two small wooden blocks, about 1 inch high, for the braces and cut one piece of wood (about 4 inches long) for the handle itself. Drill a hole through the braces as shown in the illustration on page 91. Drill a hole in the handle to match up with the braces, and drill a similar hole in the pan. Pass a bolt through the handle, brace, and pan and attach with a washer and nut. A cover may not really be necessary because you shouldn't cover a boiling brew kettle anyway.

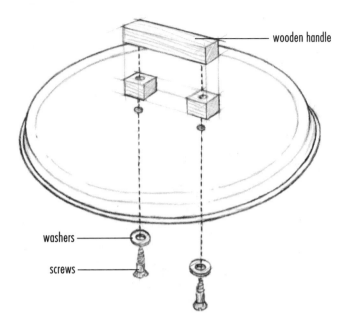

A *pizza pan*, with an easy-to-make **wooden handle**, makes a great **lid** for the modified keg brewpot.

BURNERS

Most beginning homebrewers use their kitchen stoves to boil wort. Many never get beyond that stage. The stove is easy to use and you already have it, so why worry about burners? Well, stoves are not that well suited to homebrewing. It's difficult to get many stoves (electric stoves in particular) to bring water to a vigorous boil, especially when you're dealing with batches of 7 (or 10, or 15) gallons. In addition, a large 32-quart kettle does not fit well on a stovetop, and brewing often makes a mess with boil-overs and scorched tops around the burner where the heat reflects off the pot bottom. If you're using an indoor electric stove, you'll probably find that the largest heating element is insufficient for brewing anything other than an extract batch, and that if you do a lot of batches, you'll quickly burn out the element.

One solution is to replace the heating element with a larger, higher-output element called a "canning element," which sits above the stove surface. These are available from appliance part stores for about $25. Follow the instructions that come with the burner. If your stove does not have removable electric elements, you will probably have to go with an outdoor cooker, which we discuss next.

These burners generate a lot of carbon monoxide. Always use them outdoors, or at least in a well-ventilated area. We also recommend having a carbon monoxide detector if you're using the burner in any enclosed area.

OUTDOOR COOKERS

The ideal burner for many homebrewers — especially those who are doing 10- or 15-gallon batches — is a large, outdoor propane burner.

These are inexpensive (often $30 to $50), use readily available propane, and generate enormous amounts of heat that can quickly bring large amounts of liquid to a rolling boil. The burners come with a regulator and a hose for the gas, but you'll need to buy a propane tank. If you don't already have one on your gas grill, it'll cost you about $20

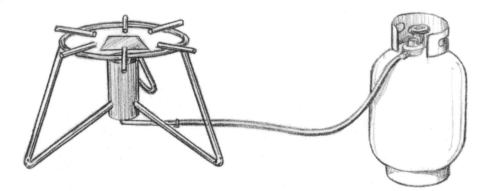

A large, outdoor **propane burner** *is ideal for homebrewing. It is inexpensive, and it heats like crazy. (Remember to check for leaks.)*

to buy a new one. Many gas stations will fill the tank for you. Alternatively, you may need to ask around or look in the phone book. These burners are available from many sources such as department stores, sporting goods dealers, and hardware stores. Some homebrew supply shops also carry the burners. Brew City Beer Gear will sell you one by mail order for about $40.

HEAT SHROUD

When using a propane cooker, you likely will notice the flame coming up around the bottom of the kettle, especially when you are just starting to heat water and the burner is set at full throttle. Indeed, there is a fair amount of heat going up along the sides of the kettle that helps the heating. If you are cooking outdoors, in an unprotected area, the wind can blow heat away from the kettle, and it will take longer to heat. A simple way to prevent this is to surround the kettle with a heat shroud. Essentially this is a piece of thin metal wrapped around the outside of the kettle, allowing the hot gas to pass between it and the kettle undisturbed.

THE PROBLEM OF SOOT

Outdoor cookers tend to create a lot of carbon soot that covers the bottom of the kettle with a plush black carpet. This can be easily removed at the end of the brewing day if you remember an old Boy Scout trick: Apply some liquid dishwashing detergent to the bottom of the pot before putting it on the heater. Excessive soot can also mean that your air-fuel mixture is not set well. A simple adjustment can often reduce soot buildup.

To make our own shroud, we shaped a piece of 18-inch-wide aluminum roof flashing into a tapered cylinder and riveted the ends together. The trick is to have the bottom of the shroud come down past, and be at least 2 inches away from, the bottom of the kettle. The flames should not touch the shroud, so you will need to know how far out the flame extends from the bottom of the kettle when the burner is set at full throttle. As long as the flame does not come in direct contact with the aluminum, there will be enough air flow to prevent it from melting. (The top of the shroud should be ½ to 1 inch away from the sides of the kettle.) You can pop-rivet standoffs to the shroud to maintain the spacing. And since you're working with aluminum, it will be easy to also make a cutout for the valve.

You will be surprised how much more rapidly the kettle heats with a shroud. With a copper brewpot and a shroud, boiling actually will begin at the sides of the kettle instead of at the bottom. In our test case, boil was achieved 5 minutes earlier, and we used a much smaller flame (than without the shroud) to maintain a rolling boil.

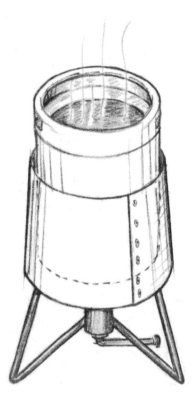

*A simple **heat shroud**, which you can make from sheet aluminum, will keep the wind out and the heat in, greatly increasing the efficiency of your burner.*

OTHER GAS BURNERS

Several burners on the market today serve homebrewers well. Many offer more precise control over the flame and are cleaner to use than the outdoor cookers. Even though these burners often have lower BTU ratings than outdoor cookers, they are perfectly capable of bringing large brew kettles to a rolling boil, precisely because they offer better control and efficiency. These burners are available — or can be adapted — for either propane or natural gas. East Coast Brewing Supply sells such a burner for $83. Superb Gas Products is also a good source for these.

WATER HEATER

Several years ago, Bill Owens published a small book entitled *How to Build a Small Brewery: Draft Beer in Ten Days.* In the first edition he advocated getting an old gas water heater, removing the heating element, and using that as a burner. In his more recent version he dropped the section on modifying a water heater in favor of recommending the inexpensive propane burners that we described previously. Bill is making the right call, but we know there are still some homebrewers who will appreciate learning that an old water-heater burner can be adapted for homebrewing. After all, gadgeteering is a hobby of many homebrewers.

ELECTRIC BREW BUCKET

In Chapter 5 we mentioned the plastic buckets with electric immersion-heating elements. These buckets can be used not only as mashing vessels but also as boilers. Bucket systems such as the Bruheat, a 220-volt model available from BrewCo, should bring 6 gallons of wort to a boil in about 40 to 50 minutes. Buckets with immersion heaters are a nice idea, but it can sometimes be difficult to get and maintain a good rolling boil.

SPOONS AND PADDLES

A spoon or paddle for stirring the boiling water is handy. Any good-quality spoon will do, either wood or stainless steel. Wood does not introduce the sanitation problem that it's sometimes made out to be because it's used in the boil, where microorganisms are killed by the heat. If you're using a slotted spoon for stirring your mash, you may want to keep a regular spoon handy for skimming the protein scum off the top of the boiling wort.

Restaurant supply shops and kitchen stores are good places to find spoons.

If you'd like to make your own wood paddle just for brewing, you can make an inexpensive one (which can also be used for stirring the mash) simply by cutting a 3-foot length of 2-inch by 6-inch hardwood lumber into a paddle, as shown in the illustration below. Use a hardwood such as oak or maple. Never use white or, especially, yellow pine, unless you like the taste of pine sap in your beer! (As we noted earlier, some homebrewers use small canoe paddles to stir large mashes.)

After cutting out the rough shape, run a sander with 80-grit sandpaper down the corners of the handle to round them over. If you've got a router and roundover bit, by all means use it! If you want to go a step further, use a belt sander to taper the thickness of the blade, but this isn't necessary. Drill a ¼-inch-diameter hole in the top of the handle so you can hang it up when you are not using the paddle.

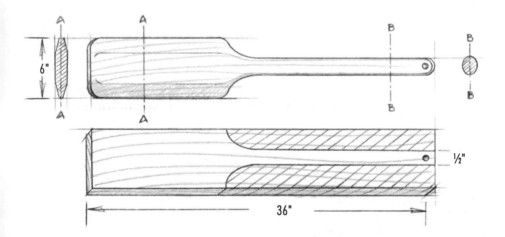

*It is easy to make **a paddle** from hardwood stock (oak or maple) for stirring the mash or boiling wort.*

HOPBACKS

The hopback is a chamber in the middle of the siphon line — between the brew kettle and the chiller — that contains fresh hops and through which you run the hot wort. This allows you to capture the fresh aromas of hops in your beer without adding them to the boil. The setup is simple: The siphon hose goes from the brew kettle to the hopback, where a second hose takes the wort to the chiller. A third hose goes from the chiller to the fermenter. Some commercial breweries, such as the Peter Austin brewhouses, use an in-line hopback like this, although they call it the "hop percolator." It's essentially the same idea. Hot wort goes into the hopback, where it is filtered through cones of fresh hops and is then pumped through the chiller and into the fermenter.

In the fall 1994 issue of *Zymurgy,* Charlie Stackhouse described how to make a simple hopback with a 10-inch length of 2-inch-diameter PVC pipe and a 2-inch-diameter stainless-steel tea ball as a filter. (A copper scrubber or stainless-steel screen also would work fine as filter material.) Begin by attaching a female-threaded end-coupler to each end of the PVC pipe. Next, insert a piece of ⅜-inch-diameter copper tube to each of two male-threaded end-cap plugs. Then jam a copper scrub pad (or fit a tea ball) into the exit (lower) end of the hopback and attach the end-plug. Finally, fill the pipe with fresh hops, attach the other end, and siphon the hot wort through. Although Stackhouse's article says to use PVC, we recommend using CPVC because PVC isn't always approved for use with food or drinking water.

Materials for a Hopback

One length of 2"-diameter PVC pipe 10" long
Two 2"-diameter end-plugs
Two 2"-diameter female-threaded end-couplers

Two lengths of ⅜"-diameter copper tubing 4" long
Filter material: stainless-steel tea ball, stainless-steel screen,
    or copper scrubber
Teflon tape
PVC cement

Directions

1. Drill a ⁵⁄₁₆"-diameter hole in each end-plug.
2. Push a piece of copper tubing into each end-plug. It's going to be a tight fit, but push just enough of the tubing to clear the inside plastic by ½".
3. Run the PVC cement applicator around one end of the 2"-diameter PVC pipe. Do the same for the smooth inside surface of one of the couplers. Push the coupler onto the tube. Do the same for the other end and allow time for the glue to harden.
4. If you're using a tea ball as your strainer, disassemble it and insert it into one of the end-plugs. You may need to file the edges of the strainer to get it to fit.
5. Wrap Teflon tape around the threads of the end-plug and install it in one of the couplers.
6. If you are using filter material, push it in from the open end until it is fully seated at the bottom of the pipe.
7. Wrap Teflon tape around the other end-plug, but wait until you are ready to use it before installing it into the open coupler.

Note: An optional hanger can be made from coat-hanger wire and a ¾"-wide piece of 2"-diameter PVC pipe. Cut a lengthwise slit in the ¾"-diameter pipe to make it into a split ring, which can be slipped over the pipe, wire hanger attached, and hung from the side of the brewpot. You could simply duct-tape the hanger to the tube, but this setup's not aesthetically pleasing. If you have a spigot on your brewpot, just attach it there.

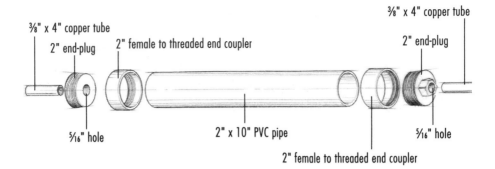

*A simple **hopback**, placed in the siphon line between the brew kettle and the chiller, allows you to capture the aromas you want in your beer.*

To use the hopback, stuff the filled hop bag into the PVC pipe, thread on the end-cap, and tighten it. Hang it on the pot. Attach the top copper tube to your racking cane with a piece of hose. Attach the bottom copper tube to your counterflow chiller (see "chillers," pages 114 to 119), and siphon the hot wort through the entire setup as usual. A siphon may not have sufficient pressure to adequately run through a hopback such as this. You may need to use a pump or other filtering technique.

SIPHONS

Many homebrewers use a dedicated copper tube to siphon the hot wort out of the kettle and into the fermenter, and you can easily make your own. Simply obtain a length of ⅜"-outside diameter copper pipe and attach a copper pot scrubber. The scrubber can be attached by drilling a small hole near the end of the siphon tube and then running a piece of wire through the hole and tying the scrubber into place. We first heard about this idea five years ago from Kinney Baughman of BrewCo. The copper scrubber (the Chore Boy brand is most commonly available) works well for filtering out hops and settled proteins. The best way to do this is to vigorously stir the wort before siphoning so that the settled material gathers toward the center of the pot; and then insert the siphon tube with the copper scrubber attached and start the siphon.

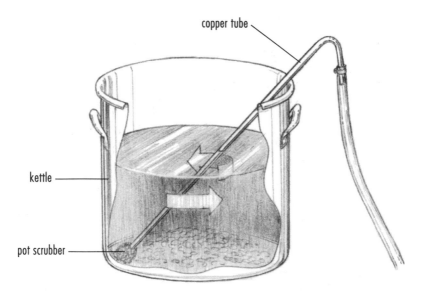

*A **copper tube** can be used to siphon hot wort from the brewkettle to the fermenter. A **copper pot scrubber** attached to the end of the tube works great for filtering out hops and sediment.*

–7–

CHILLING
THE WORT

Wort boils at a temperature of over 200°F, yet yeast cannot be pitched (i.e., added) at much over 80°F. This means that you need to cool the hot wort considerably — to a temperature at which the yeast can thrive.

Some homebrewers want their beers cooled down to below 60°F. They do this for two reasons. First, cooling beer to below 60°F enables brewers to achieve a more effective cold break, the point at which suspended proteins drop out of suspension as the wort is cooled. A good cold break can produce a clearer, more brilliant beer. Second, lager yeasts work best at cooler temperatures, so the beer is left to ferment at temperatures in the below-50°F range.

Several methods of chilling are available to homebrewers. The best method for your home brewery will depend to a large extent on the types of beer you are producing, the methods you're most comfortable with, or even personal bias — yours or the people advising you at the local homebrew supply shop! Some of the more common methods for cooling include:

✔ Dilution of wort
✔ Immersion of pot in water or ice
✔ Counterflow chiller
✔ Immersion chiller

SIMPLE CHILLING METHODS FOR EXTRACT BREWERS

Because most extract brewers tend to do smaller-scale boils — typically 2 gallons — they rely on dilution or placing the pot in an ice-water bath to chill the wort. All-grain brewers always do full-scale boils, so they must use methods that rely on some form of heat exchange (extracting heat from the wort and removing it) to cool their beer. (This will be discussed in the next section.)

Dilution and Simple Chilling Methods

Let's begin by looking at ways by which extract brewers chill small batches. Many introductory homebrewing texts advocate boiling only a small amount of the total water needed for a batch of beer — usually 6 quarts. That leaves 14 quarts that can be used to dilute and cool the concentrated wort — actually it's a bit less because you're adding malt extract to the 6 quarts. This will work fine if your water is cold enough — and it will have to be very cold for this to work. In many parts of the country, however, tap water is often at 60°F or warmer, especially in the summer months; and 14 quarts of water at this temperature will not cool 6 quarts of boiling water to a temperature that will allow you to pitch yeast. Therefore you need to add a step to chill the wort properly.

wort

ice

Chilling wort. *The simplest but least effective way to chill your wort is to set your brewpot into a sink full of ice water.*

One method that works fairly well for small batches is to set the brewpot in a sink full of ice water and stir both the ice water and the wort (see the illustration). This method does not carry heat away from the wort efficiently, so you may need to add ice to the bath continuously. But if you stick with it, you should be able to lower the wort temperature close enough to pitching temperature so that, combined with dilution, the wort cools adequately.

Cooling works most effectively when there is a large temperature difference between the liquid you're trying to cool and the liquid you're using to cool it. Accordingly, many homebrewers have wondered why nobody recommends adding ice directly to the hot wort. The reason: Freezing temperatures do not kill bacteria or other microorganisms that might infect the beer. In fact, adding ice directly to the wort is a good way to *cause* an infection. Maybe not this time, but eventually it will catch up with you.

That said, adding one 8-pound bag of ice to 6 quarts of boiled wort will lower its temperature enough so that diluting with water (even at 60°F) should get you to just about the right temperature for pitching. Store-bought ice from a dedicated ice freezer is probably better than ice you make yourself. In the *Homebrewer's Companion,* however, Charlie Papazian suggests that you can freeze ice somewhat safely by putting water in a zip-sealing bag and then putting that bag in a second zip-sealing bag. Adding ice to the wort is effective but is generally not a good practice. If anybody asks, we didn't tell you to do it — we told you to build a wort chiller.

CHILLER TYPES AND AN INTRODUCTION TO HEAT EXCHANGE

What factors are important when you consider buying or building a wort chiller?

Effectiveness. You want to make sure that the chiller can actually drop the temperature to the proper level. If you are concerned about cold break, you want to drop the temperature below your ideal pitching temperature.

Sanitation. You need to keep the chiller free of bacteria that might infect your beer.

Speed. You want the chilling operation completed quickly, not just because you want to get on with it but because wort exposed to the air during a slow temperature drop is prone to airborne infections.

Construction and ease of use. What good is an effective design if it's hard to use or requires special skills or tools to build?

Cost. Of course, we would like a great chiller at a low cost. Dollars matter to most of us.

There are generally two types of wort chillers: immersion chillers and counterflow chillers. In an immersion chiller, liquid of one temperature flows through a coil that is immersed in liquid of another temperature. The difference in temperature causes the heat to move from the hot liquid to the cool liquid. This is how heat exchange works — a cool liquid absorbs and carries away the heat energy from the hot liquid.

Counterflow chillers also rely on heat transfer from the hot liquid to the cool, which carries away the heat (although it may no longer be very cool once it absorbs heat). In a counterflow chiller, the two liquids flow in opposite directions — typically by running the hot wort through a thin copper tube that is encased in a larger tube that carries cold water. Two important advantages of counterflow chillers are: (1) they are closed systems, so the beer is never exposed to the air during cooling, and (2) they chill the wort very rapidly. Wort can be prone to infection if it drops in temperature slowly; but when it is chilled rapidly in a closed system, there is significantly less risk of infection than with immersion chillers. With good sanitation practices, the counterflow chiller is the technically superior approach.

IMMERSION CHILLERS

Immersion chillers are usually built from a coil of copper tubing with connectors on each end to which hoses are attached (garden hoses are often used). One connector is run to a source of cold water; the other is run to a drain for expelling the hot water. The immersion chiller offers a simple, effective way to quickly cool hot wort.

Basic Immersion Chiller

Chillers are readily available from many homebrew supply shops for $30 to $35; however, they can also be built at home for a bit less than that. One advantage to building the chiller yourself is that you can adapt the plans to suit your own needs. We'll describe a few ways that chillers can be adapted to work more effectively.

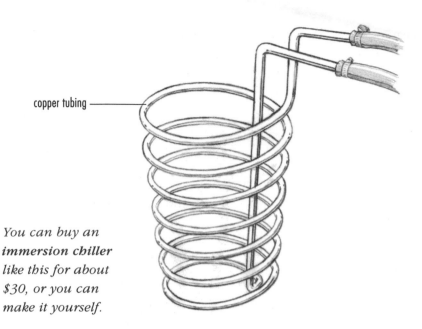

copper tubing

You can buy an immersion chiller like this for about $30, or you can make it yourself.

When you build a wort chiller, the most critical aspect is the tubing you choose. Copper works well because it efficiently transmits heat energy and is readily available at fairly low cost. Stainless-steel tubing would work, but it costs more. Aluminum also works fine, but some brewers feel that it tends to give the beer a metallic taste. There is, however, no real evidence of such flavor problems. Your tubing should be ⅜-inch in diameter. If you use a thinner tube, you will achieve potentially greater efficiency because the thinner tube will give you more surface area per volume. However, chillers made from ¼-inch-diameter tubing tend to take much longer to cool wort and are prone to clogging. Using ⅜-inch-diameter tubing gives you good efficiency and acceptable cooling times, and it avoids clogging.

Materials for a Wort Chiller

25' of ⅜"-diameter copper tubing
Two hose clamps
One inexpensive garden hose (25' is all you need)

Note: Lengths of copper tubing greater than 20' usually come in a large coil. Most hardware stores will want to sell you a full box containing 50' to 60' of tubing. Shop with a friend and build two wort chillers if your hardware store will not sell you a cut length (or maybe find a new hardware store!). You could also build two chillers and use the double-coil chiller method that we describe on page 111 and 112.

Note: Before you begin, you should know that you can easily crimp your copper tubing and ruin that section of it. Once it's crimped, cut out the crimped section and attach a coupler by soldering (lead-free, please). If you don't have a spring tubing bender, buy one when you buy your copper tubing. It will help make the 90 degree bends without crimping the tubing.

One other point: You should plan to leave enough copper tubing on the ends so that they stick out over the sides of the pot (see illustration on page 108). Once in a while you may get leaks from loose hose clamps; if the tubing-hose connection is outside the pot and it does leak, the water will not drip into the wort.

Directions

1. Turn the copper tubing into a coil, as shown in the illustration on page 108. If the tubing came as a large coil, you can wind it into a tighter coil by hand. This is done by holding one end and turning the coils into ever-smaller coils. If you have a soda keg handy, simply wrap the tubing around that. Leave about 18" to 24" on one end. The final diameter must be small enough so there is at least 2" between the interior sides of the brewpot and the coil.

2. Bend the short end of the tube at the top of the coil 90 degrees out from the coil.

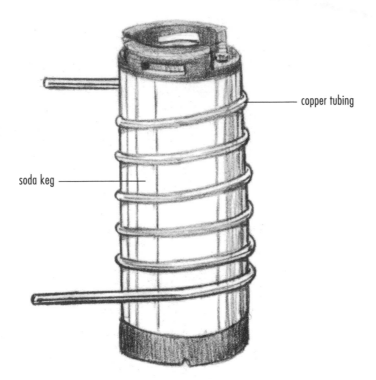

copper tubing

soda keg

*You can coil the **copper tubing** for your **immersion chiller** by wrapping it carefully around a soda keg.*

3. Bend the longer end 90 degrees so that the length of the tube goes back up toward the top of the coil.
4. Bend the top part of the long length out from the coil.
5. Cut the garden hose so that each length is at least 5' or 6' long.
6. Slide a clamp over each cut end of the hose.
7. Slip one hose length over one end of the coil. Repeat with the other hose at the other end of the coil.
8. Tighten the clamps to hold the hose lengths firmly to the coil.

That's it! Your immersion chiller is ready to use, and it should have cost you less than $25.

We recommend testing the chiller before brewing a batch of beer, just to convince yourself that everything works and to satisfy yourself that there will be no surprises when the time comes to press the chiller into service. We tested our chillers by boiling a brewpot full of water, to which we had added ½ gallon of vinegar, and seeing how long it would take to cool it. The vinegar is important because it will clean the outside of the chiller and prepare it for use in the wort.

In addition to the chiller, you will need a hose that's long enough to run from your faucet to the chiller. If you're using the chiller in your kitchen, as most people do, you may need to twist off the end of your faucet to reveal the threads. These threads should accept a standard hose fitting, but many kitchen faucets need a threaded adapter to accept a hose connection.

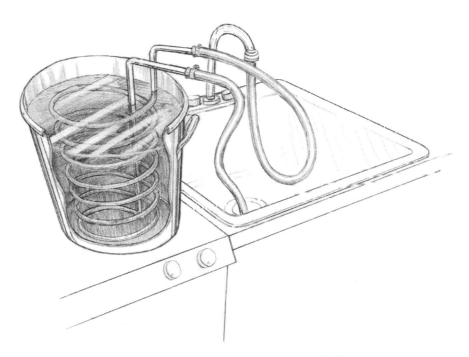

*When you are ready to use your new **immersion chiller**, sanitize it by putting it into the boil for 15 to 20 minutes. When the boil is done, attach the hoses — and chill out.*

These are available at most hardware stores for $1 to $2. Some homebrew supply shops also sell the adapters. If you can't get the end of your faucet off, or if you just don't want to mess with it, you can buy a rubber adapter that will fit over the end of the faucet, avoiding the need to unscrew the faucet sprayer. One of these adapters is the shower hose attachment that Jack Schmidling Productions includes with the EasySparger.

Our chiller has one length of hose long enough to run from our sink faucet to the brewpot, and another long enough to carry the heated water to the drain. The typical chiller from a homebrew supply shop comes with lengths of hose that are only a few inches to a foot in length. You could make your hose lengths that short on this chiller too, but if you do, you will need to get two more hoses to use when brewing to carry the water to the chiller and then to carry the hot waste water back to your drain. Keep an eye on the end of the hose in the sink, or use something to hold it in place. A loose hose end can make a real mess. By using long lengths of hose, we've avoided the need for extra hoses, although our chiller is a bit more cumbersome to store. As we've said before, homebrewing equipment and gadgets always involve trade-offs.

When you're ready to use the chiller, sanitize it by setting it down into your brewpot 15 to 20 minutes before the end of the boil. The heat will destroy any bacteria or other microorganisms on its surfaces. Then when the boil is done, simply attach the hose to your faucet, set the other end of the hose in the sink, and turn on the faucet. Five gallons of wort should cool from boiling to below 80°F in about 15 to 20 minutes. The time will depend on the flow rate and temperature of the water.

Another way to use the immersion chiller is to put the chiller in a second vessel (a large fermenting bucket works well) and then run the wort through the chiller and drain it into the fermenter. (This was described in *Zymurgy*, Spring 1992, page 38.) If you do this, you will need to modify your chiller.

We do not recommend running the wort through the immersion chiller. Although some homebrewers believe it is largely a matter of choice as to whether to run the wort through the chiller, or run water through the chiller, there are a number of factors that argue against running wort through the chiller. The most important is sanitation. You will have more sanitation problems with this approach because you will need to sanitize the inside of the tube thoroughly before and after each batch to prevent infections. Indeed, it is much easier to keep the outside of a tube clean than the inside.

Immersing the chiller in the wort is a simpler and more straightforward method, even though it is relatively inefficient in its use of water. If you still want to run wort through the chiller, the counterflow chiller is a better solution.

One idea worth considering is to build a wort chiller that is capable of doubling as a jockey box, so that you can use one gadget for two purposes. (The jockey box is an ice chest through which beer lines run, cooling it for drinking. We'll describe how to build a jockey box in Chapter 10.) To adapt this device for use as a wort chiller, you simply need to attach hoses to the in and out stems on the jockey box, fill the box with ice, and siphon the wort through.

Double-Coil Immersion Chiller

If you are worried about wasting water, want faster cooling times, or have a cold-water supply that just isn't cold enough, you can build a chiller with two coils that are connected by a length of hose. Set one coil in a bath of ice water, the other coil in the hot wort, and then run water through the chiller. This is more efficient because (1) you are cooling the water before it gets to the brewpot, and (2) you are using a single coil with a greater difference in temperature between the cooling fluid and the wort. Thus the heat-exchange process works more efficiently, that is, the cold water has more potential to absorb heat energy. The illustration below shows an example of this kind of chiller.

Materials for a Double-Coil Immersion Chiller

50' of ⅜" O.D. (outside diameter) copper tubing
One inexpensive garden hose
One length of ⅜" I.D. (inside diameter) plastic tubing
Four hose clamps

Build the chiller as described in the instructions on pages 106 to 108; however, this time you will need to build two coils instead of one, and you will need to run the plastic tubing between the two coils, attaching it with the clamps.

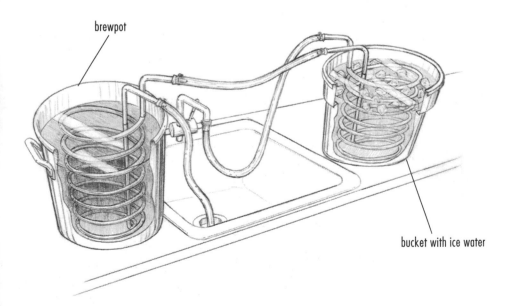

brewpot

bucket with ice water

Double-coil chiller. This one calls for two coils, the first to lower the temperature of the cold water, the second to chill the wort.

Making the Basic Chiller into a Super Chiller

If you want to get the benefits of the double-coil chiller without the added cost of building a second coil (since copper can be quite expensive), simply pump the ice water directly through the single coil. Although this will typically require some kind of pump, a pump may be cheaper than a second coil, especially if you're able to find one at a yard sale. You can use a chiller with a standard utility pump that you can pick up for less than $30 at a hardware store. Using this method, we dropped our chilling time down to about 12 minutes. Another advantage of this method is that — potentially — you can chill the wort much further, giving yourself either a lower pitching temperature or a better cold break.

Alternate Designs for Immersion Chillers

Most immersion chillers on the market have coils arranged vertically, like an extended spring. This approach tends to maximize the area of hot wort that is being chilled, but it's by no means the only way to design a chiller. Phil Fleming has an interesting

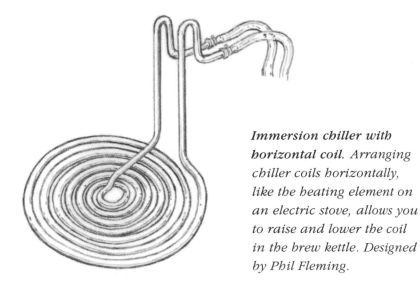

Immersion chiller with horizontal coil. Arranging chiller coils horizontally, like the heating element on an electric stove, allows you to raise and lower the coil in the brew kettle. Designed by Phil Fleming.

design in which the coils are tightly woven horizontally, like the burner on an electric stove. According to Phil, this allows you to raise or lower the chiller coil to maximize cooling at a specific layer of wort. His idea was described in the *Zymurgy* special issue of 1992.

COUNTERFLOW CHILLERS

As we noted earlier, if you want to run wort through your chiller, a counterflow chiller is the best way to go. We'll describe several you can build yourself.

PVC Pipe Counterflow Chiller

The PVC pipe counterflow chiller is one of the more popular counterflow chiller designs to emerge over the last several years. It is fairly simple to build and use, and it works faster than most immersion setups. However, as with all counterflow chillers, the

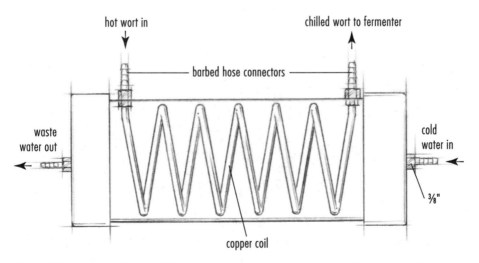

*The **PVC counterflow chiller** (cutaway view) allows cold water to flow through a section of large-diameter plastic pipe, while hot wort circulates through the small-diameter copper coil installed inside the plastic pipe. See illustration on p. 116 for another view of the PVC counterflow chiller.*

inside of the copper tubing needs to be cleaned carefully before and after use because any trace of beer left behind can lead to infection.

The PVC pipe chiller involves taking a 2-foot length of a large-diameter PVC pipe; inserting a copper coil inside; drilling two holes, one for bringing in cold water and another for expelling hot water; attaching fittings for water hoses; and then sealing the ends. To use: Pump hot wort through the coil while simultaneously pumping cold water through the pipe.

Materials for a PVC Pipe Counterflow Chiller

One 2'-length of 6" PVC pipe
Two PVC pipe caps (also called "end-caps")
Four ⅜" compression x ⅜" MPT adapters
10' of ⅜" copper tubing
Four ½" hose barb x ⅜" FPT connectors
½" heat-resistant hose
½" PVC hose
25' inexpensive garden hose, ½" diameter
PVC cement
Epoxy cement
Teflon tape

Directions

1. Drill a ½"-diameter hole in each end-cap.
2. Insert the compression end of a ⅜" compression x ⅜" MPT adapter into each end-cap and seal with epoxy.
3. Drill a ½"-diameter hole 2" from both ends of the PVC pipe.
4. Coil the copper tubing and insert it into the PVC pipe.
5. Place a compression nut and ferrule on each end of the coil.
6. Insert the compression end of a ⅜" compression x ⅜" MPT adapter into each hole in the PVC pipe.

7. Thread the compression nuts onto the adapters and tighten. Seal the adapters with epoxy cement.

8. Coat the inside rim of an end-cap and the outside of one end of the PVC pipe with PVC cement. Place end-cap on pipe and repeat for other end. Be sure all sealing surfaces are evenly coated with the PVC cement to avoid leaks.

9. Wrap a couple turns of Teflon tape around each ⅜" MPT, thread on the hose barbs, and lightly tighten. Do *not* overtighten.

10. Add the hoses and you're done!

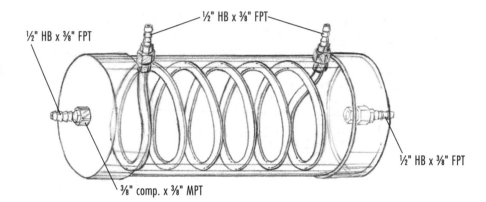

½" HB x ⅜" FPT

½" HB x ⅜" FPT

½" HB x ⅜" FPT

⅜" comp. x ⅜" MPT

*The **PVC counterflow chiller** (completed) is one of the most popular means of chilling wort. The key to success, however, is making sure you sanitize the inside of the copper tubing.*

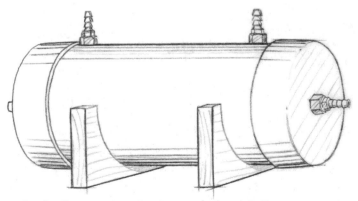

*If you've built your own PVC counterflow chiller, you might also consider making a **wooden stand** for it.*

You may want to build a small stand for the chiller using strips of wood (see illustration on page 116). Otherwise the pipe has a tendency to move around. You can either cut a rounded curve in two end pieces, or you can build a four-sided rack — whatever works for you.

Another method for "controlling" your chiller is to wrap a length of 16-gauge wire around the pipe just below one end-cap and twist the ends into a double wire. Bend the end lengths 90 degrees up past the end-cap, make a hook, and hang it from the brewpot handle. Use your imagination and remember: the simpler, the better.

Karl once visited a homebrewer whose setup could be described as "A stand for everything, and everything in its stand!" Literally every piece of apparatus had some kind of metal stand. The over-kill was undoubtedly the adjustable PVC pipe chiller stand made from uni-strut material. The pipe chiller could be adjusted up and down in the stand, but when asked if the chiller ever moved, the owner answered with a meek "No."

If you prefer, you can replace the water in and water out hose barbs with hose fittings. This will allow you to disconnect the water supply hoses and make storage much simpler. You will need: one ¾" male hose to ⅜" FPT adapter and one ¾" female hose to ⅜" FPT adapter.

Simply replace the barbs with the hose adapters. The female hose adapter should be on the water inlet of the chiller. When you're ready to use the chiller, you can attach one garden hose to one end and another garden hose to the other end. Some people don't want to mess about hooking up lots of stuff, and others don't like storage problems. As we said earlier, trade-offs abound in homebrewing.

Hose Counterflow Chiller

In the hose counterflow chiller, a copper tube is inserted inside a standard garden hose and the wort is pumped, or siphoned, so that it runs in a direction opposite to the water flow.

Before we delve into a description of making a chiller from scratch, we need to mention that the tube fittings can be bought already made. These fittings are produced by Listermann

Manufacturing and are sold under the name "Phil's Phittings." This fitting kit sells for about $15 and really makes building a chiller easy work.

Materials for a Hose Counterflow Chiller

50' of ⅝" I.O. (inside diameter) garden hose
50' of ⅜" O.D. (outside diameter) soft copper tubing
Six 1½"-long pieces of ½" copper pipe
Two ½" copper tees
Two ½" copper end-caps
Six hose clamps
Plastic zip ties or wire

Directions

1. Cut off 8" from each end of the hose and save for Step 9.
2. Insert a ½"-long copper pipe into each end of the copper tees and solder them in place.
3. Drill a ⅜"-diameter hole in the end of each copper end-cap. (Hint: Start with a ⅛" drill and work up to a ⅜" drill.)
4. Place an end-cap on one end of the long leg of the tees and solder into place.
5. Uncoil the copper tubing and feed it through the garden hose.
6. Place a hose clamp on both ends of the hose.
7. Feed the end of the copper tubing through the tee assembly and onto the hose, then tighten clamp. Repeat for other end.
8. Solder the ⅜" tubing to the end-caps to seal.
9. Attach the hose ends to the short legs of the tees with hose clamps.
10. Wind the hose and tubing assembly into a coil around a large cylinder such as your brewpot.
11. Secure the coils together with wire or zip ties.

12. To sanitize the chiller before using it for the first time, run a very hot solution of 75 percent water and 25 percent vinegar through the copper tubing.

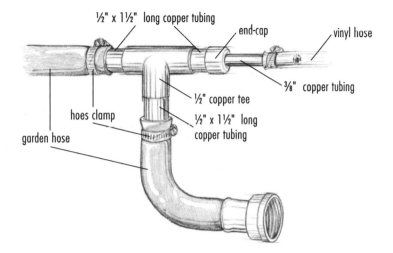

½" x 1½" long copper tubing

end-cap

vinyl hose

⅜" copper tubing

½" copper tee

hoes clamp

½" x 1½" long copper tubing

garden hose

*In a **hose counterflow chiller**, a copper tube is inserted in a garden hose. Water flows through the hose (and over the tube) in one direction, while hot wort is pumped through the tube in the opposite direction. This is how the plumbing is set up.*

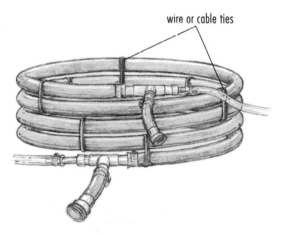

wire or cable ties

*A **hose counterflow chiller** coiled up and ready for action.*

COMMERCIALLY AVAILABLE CHILLERS

There are a number of wort chillers on the market, and many are very good products. Immersion chillers made from a simple coil of copper tubing with garden-hose adapters are available at most homebrew supply shops for about $30 to $40. If you can't find one locally, they are also available from The Home Brewery for $29.95 (as of early 1995). Although these chillers often use garden-hose fittings, The Home Brewery also sells an adapter for attaching it to a kitchen sink. The adapters are available at hardware stores as well.

BrewCo offers a counterflow chiller for $70; several other companies offer similar counterflow chillers for about the same price. Heart's Home Beer & Wine Making Supply sells a very nice helical (coiled) unit for $70. Stoelting sells a counterflow chiller for about $170 that has copper fins on the stainless-steel inner tube to better conduct heat from the hot wort to the cold coolant.

Brewers Warehouse sells an immersion chiller that includes a copper racking tube. For the most serious homebrewers and small-scale professional brewers, they also sell a chiller unit that includes a pump, rolling cart, and oxygenator for $900.

Of the commercially available chillers, the one we like best is the helical chiller from Heart's Home Beer & Wine. However, if you're looking to save some money, the immersion chiller from The Home Brewery is an excellent value.

SUMMARY

As with all equipment and procedures in homebrewing, the choice of chilling method is up to you. The way you chill your wort depends on your own setup and your own biases and a weighing of the options based on cost, difficulty of using or constructing, storage space, and many other considerations.

Chiller type	Pros	Cons
Immersion chiller	• Cheap and easy to build • Easy to clean • Cold break material is left in pot	• Wort is exposed the entire time • Easy to introduce hot side aeration if moved about too violently
Double coil immersion chiller	• Relatively inexpensive and cools more rapidly than a single coil • Cold break material is left in pot	• Same problem as above, plus the added complexity of a second coil • Extra container and storage space required • Needs a supply of ice
Immersion chiller with pump	• Cools more rapidly than single coil • Cold break material is left in pot	• Same problems as single immersion chiller, but about the same complexity as double coil • Requires ice, extra container, and electricity
PVC pipe counterflow chiller	• Cost is similar to double coil • Wort is not exposed to air • Can be oriented in different ways • Self-contained unit	• Coil must be thoroughly rinsed and sanitized before and after every use • Cold break material goes into fermenter • More complicated and time-consuming to build
Hose counterflow chiller	• Cost is less than PVC pipe chiller • Wort is not exposed to air • Can be oriented in different ways • Self-contained unit	• All the problems of the PVC pipe chiller, plus aesthetically not very appealing and less compact • Easier to damage coil than PVC pipe chiller
Bucket in ice	• The winner of the Cheapness and Simplicity award • Cold break material is left in pot	• Slow • Cold break not as good as with chillers • Only works well for volumes under 2 gallons • Needs lots of ice

In our opinion, the best combination of performance and price is the basic immersion chiller. It is easy to make, simple to use, and very easy to clean. You do not need to worry about cleaning the inside of the tube because all you're running through it is cooling water, which ultimately goes down the drain.

– 8 –

FERMENTERS

THE FERMENTER IS A VESSEL in which the yeast consumes sugars, converting them to alcohol, carbon dioxide, and various flavor components. Not only does the fermenter serve as a container for the liquid, but it also provides an environment that encourages healthy and vigorous yeast growth. Therefore, when we buy or build a fermenter we need to consider the temperature range at which yeast works, how bacterial or other infections occur (and how to prevent such infections), and how other aspects of the fermenter (e.g., material or shape) can affect fermentation.

OPEN AND CLOSED FERMENTATION

Most basic homebrewing texts recommend a fermentation approach known as "closed fermentation" in which the fermenter is sealed to prevent airborne contaminants — such as bacteria or wild yeasts — from entering the beer and producing off flavors. In the home brewery, this is done by placing a lid on the

*Homebrewers can use a stainless-steel kettle as an **open fermenter.** Cover is used after kraeusen falls.*

fermenting bucket or putting a cap on the carboy, but with an airlock mechanism to allow CO_2 to escape. Closed fermentation is the method used by most homebrewers (and by most commercial breweries). However, fermentation does not have to be done that way.

With open fermentation, the beer is not sealed in an air-tight container. Many traditional commercial breweries use open fermenters, exposing the actively fermenting beer to the open air. Homebrewers can do this simply by using a brewpot as a fermenter. In fact, you can use a single pot for mashing, boiling, and fermenting. But if you choose to do open fermentation in your home brewery, you need to use a pot that is at least 5 quarts larger than your batch size. This is because the fermenting yeast will kick up a head of foam at high kraeusen, and you'll need to allow it room to expand. Pitching high volumes of yeast is critical with open fermenters. (You should also leave the cover on the pot most of the time, especially during the yeast's initial growth period and after the kraeusen drops. You can crack the lid during high kraeusen.)

SINGLE-STAGE AND TWO-STAGE FERMENTATION

Single-stage fermentation means that the entire fermentation process is conducted in a single vessel. Two-stage means that one vessel is used for the initial fermentation, where most of the vigorous activity occurs, and then the beer is transferred to a second vessel to finish the fermentation. Single-stage fermentation is simple and requires little equipment. Two-stage fermentation is usually preferred by experienced brewers because it removes the beer from settled hops, proteins, and dead yeast, creating a cleaner flavor. It also reduces sediment, giving you a clearer beer.

AIRLOCKS AND BLOW-OFF TUBES

Critical to any closed-fermentation system is the airlock or blow-off tube. Without this, the fermenter would build up pressure and explode. The airlock or blow-off tube allows CO_2 to escape while preventing airborne contaminants from entering the fermenter. The illustration on page 126 shows several types of airlocks and blow-off schemes. In this section we'll talk about using blow-off tubes and working with rubber stoppers for carboys. There's really no reason to make an airlock (other than a blow-off tube) because they're inexpensive. Every homebrew or wine-making supplier has them, and they're more trouble to make than the pocket change it would take to buy one.

Some older homebrewing textbooks recommended attaching small vinyl hoses (⅜-inch) to the nipple attachments on a carboy cap. These hoses were far too small and often clogged from sticky trub (sediment), hop particles or whole cones, yeast, or fruit solids. In most cases pressure built up in the carboy and sent the cap skyward, followed by a geyser of beer and foam. Occasionally some homebrewers even experienced a shattered carboy, which could be dangerous. So, if you use blow-off tubes

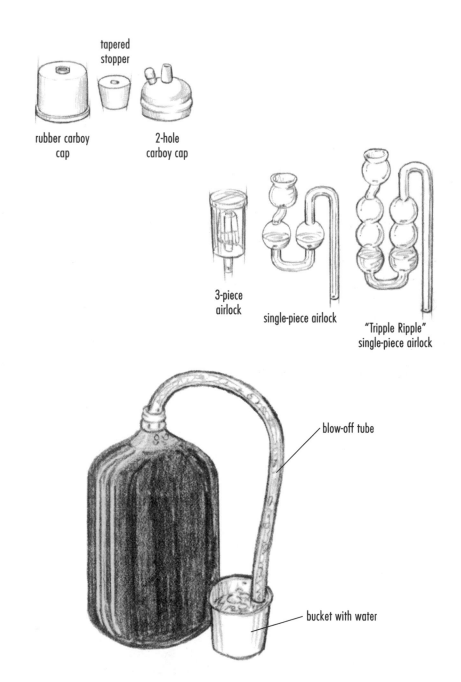

Airlocks and *blow-off tubes* prevent closed fermentation systems from exploding by allowing CO_2 to escape. They also prevent contaminants from entering the fermenter.

— and blow-off tubes do work well to remove trub from the beer — then make sure you use a large tube. The best approach is to use a very large hose (say, 1 inch or 1½ inches in diameter — just measure the opening in your carboy; the inner diameter of the mouth is the outer diameter of the hose you want).

RUBBER STOPPERS

Most homebrew supply shops sell carboy caps made from molded plastic, and these are really handy and probably the best choice for most homebrewers. However, you can easily use rubber stoppers. You want the drilled stoppers, if available. Otherwise you've got to drill a hole in the rubber and you'll quickly find that a drill bit does not work. A better approach is to make a hole driller from a length of brass tube.

Directions for a Hole Driller

1. Get a tube with an outer diameter that's the same as the inner diameter of the hole you want.
2. Cut the tube to about 4 inches.

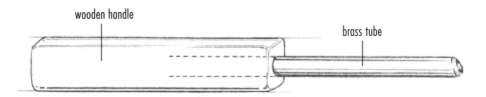

*You can easily make this **hole driller** for putting holes in rubber carboy stoppers.*

3. Drill a hole about halfway through a small length of 1 x 2 or a similar sized piece of wood (see the illustration on page 127). This wood will be your handle.
4. Now put some adhesive in the hole and insert the brass tube.
5. Cut the tube at an angle to form a point. Sharpen the entire rounded edge of the tube with a file. (A grinder or a grinder attachment for a drill will clog up quickly with the soft brass, lessening the effectiveness of the grinder. Also, it is very difficult to remove the brass from small grinders.)
6. Now your hole driller is done! Push it into the rubber stopper with a turning motion. Pretty nifty, eh?

TEMPERATURE CONTROL

Each yeast strain has an optimal temperature range within which it grows and reproduces at just the right rate for homebrewing. When a yeast strain grows too quickly, it produces more undesirable by-products (flavor compounds) such as esters, higher alcohols, and diacetyl. The key to fermentation, therefore, as in almost everything concerning brewing, is balance. The temperature should be warm enough for the yeast to reproduce well but not so high as to encourage rapid growth.

For most ale strains, the optimal temperature will be in the range of 60°F to 68°F. Yes, ale yeasts reproduce much more quickly as the temperature goes above 70°F, but they are also more likely to produce undesirable flavors. Controlled growth, not unfettered rapid growth, is the goal. Most lager strains work best from about 45°F to the low 50°F range.

The problem most homebrewers face is how to keep the fermenter cool, especially for lager strains. But quite a few homebrewers who rely on naturally cool environments (such as cellars) often worry about keeping the fermenter warm. These brewers need some kind of heating device to keep the environment at an appropriate temperature. Other brewers have to deal with highly variable environments (such as garages in mountainous areas where nighttime temperatures drop quickly). These people must provide both adequate cooling and heating to maintain a constant temperature. The key for all brewers is consistency; wide temperature fluctuations cause problems.

KEEPING THE FERMENTER COOL

The biggest problem most homebrewers face is keeping the fermenter cool enough. They use a number of different methods to solve this problem. The simplest approach is to find an area in your house that maintains a consistent temperature in the appropriate range. In a home that is warmed in winter months to a temperature of 68 to 70°F, an outside corner closet may never get above 65°F. Look for these corners because they represent the easiest and most trouble-free way to keep your beer happily fermenting. Basements often are excellent choices, but not all homes have basements, and in some climates an unheated basement may be too cold for some yeast strains. In this case you may want to consider brewing a type of beer that does work well at the available temperature.

Warm summer months, however, are anathema to clean-tasting beers, and often you need to take action. Among the approaches we describe here are using water evaporation, refrigeration, and ice baths to cool a fermenter. We'll start with the low-tech solutions and work our way up to approaches with higher "gadgetude" quotients.

The Wet Towel Approach

You may be able to harness the cooling properties of water evaporation to cool your fermenter a few degrees. This method will drop the fermenter temperature only about 5 degrees (some

Cooling the fermenter. A T-shirt, a fan, and a large tray filled with water, and you're ready to cool your carboy through evaporation.

authors have claimed to drop the temperature 10 degrees with this method), and that may be enough to keep your beer clean-tasting, especially if you live in a home with air-conditioning.

Here's how to do it: Get a large tray and set your carboy in it. A cat litter box works well, as does a sandbox or a small children's wading pool. Fill the tray with cool water. Soak a towel, T-shirt, or other piece of absorbent cloth in the water and then drape it over the carboy with one end remaining in the water.

Absorbent cloth will act like a wick and carry the water from the tray to wet the entire material area. Then, as the water evaporates, it carries away heat from the fermenter. Relying only on evaporation, however, will not drop the temperature more than a couple of degrees. To drop the temperature by 5 degrees you will need (1) to position the fermenter near an air-conditioning duct that blows air across the wet towel, or (2) to place a small fan nearby to blow air across the towel, encouraging rapid evaporation. Periodically you should check the water level to make sure that water is available for evaporation. Some brewers have found that the towel may also develop mold. If this happens, replace the towel often. Chlorine bleach may inhibit the mold, but it will also discolor your towel.

The Cold Bath Water Approach

Some homebrewers with air-conditioned houses are able to drop the fermentation a few degrees (usually about the same amount as with the wet towel) by leaving the fermenter in a bathtub filled with cool water and, several times daily, inserting a block of ice to cool the water. The idea is that instead of trying to carry the heat energy away from the fermenter, the heat is diluted into a larger volume of water and the water temperature is periodically lowered by adding ice.

One homebrewer we know uses this method regularly. He keeps a couple of plastic gallon jugs of water frozen in his freezer and simply adds one to the bathtub in the evening and another in the morning. He rotates the two jugs between the freezer and the bathtub and reports that he keeps his fermenter about 3 degrees cooler than it would be normally.

This is not a method that we favor because it requires frequent temperature monitoring, and it is inefficient. Not only does the method require making a lot of ice, but the temperature drop is not enough for many homebrewers' purposes. We mention it here only because it works for some folks and helps keep our eye on the perspective that simple is usually better.

Refrigerators and Freezers

Most serious homebrewers, and those who like gadgets, prefer using a dedicated refrigerator or freezer to maintain the fermentation temperature. This method is the most reliable and is independent of environmental circumstances — refrigeration works just as well in Arizona as in Maine. Further, because refrigerators are insulated, the energy used to cool the fermenter is focused on the fermenter — you're not cooling more area than you need. If you adapt a refrigerator for this purpose, you've also got a good place to store kegs of beer — but we'll get to that later.

Refrigerators and freezers are also easy to come by. Almost everyone will, in the course of a year, run into a relative, co-worker, or neighbor who wants to replace his working, but ugly or featureless, refrigerator with a newer model. If not, just browse the want ads in a local paper or even run an ad yourself telling the readers that you'll take an old fridge off their hands. In no case would we pay more than about $40 for an old refrigerator — they're just too easy to find. Used appliance dealers are generally not a very good source of old refrigerators because they charge too much. Do not buy a nonworking refrigerator unless you have a refrigeration expert in the family or one who owes you a favor or will work for homebrew. The cost of repairing could be far more than you bargained for.

Should you use a refrigerator or a freezer? Well, if you've got a choice, go for the freezer; it will cool down to a lower temperature. Refrigerators often are not intended to cool below about 40°F, and some we've seen have had trouble maintaining lager temperatures in warm summer months.

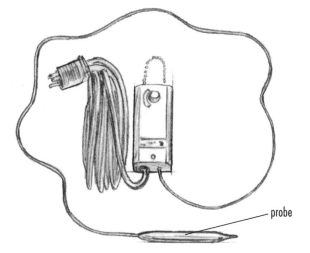

There are a variety of **thermostats** *available for controlling the temperature of your refrigerator.*

probe

To adapt a refrigerator or freezer for use as a fermenter cold room, you will need a thermostat controller. Thermostats in refrigerators will not accept the range of temperatures you need to use for beer (I don't know of any that would let you ferment an ale at 65°F and a lager at 33°F).

The thermostats used by homebrewers to control refrigerators are usually the kind used to control room air-conditioners. These are available from most hardware stores or from heating and air-conditioning suppliers. Most homebrewers seem to prefer

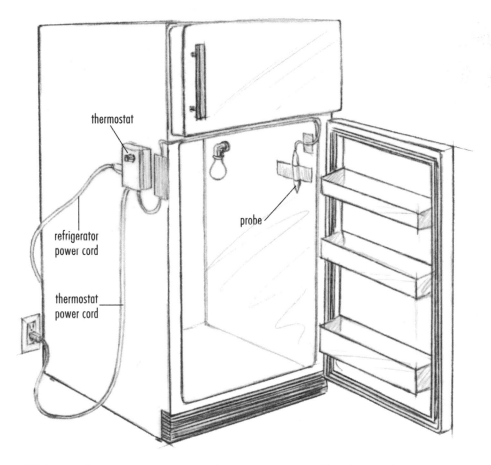

Wiring a thermostat to your refrigerator is easy: The thermostat plugs into a wall outlet. The refrigerator plugs into the thermostat, and a probe from the thermostat is place inside the refrigerator to monitor the temperature.

the Hunter Airstat or the Hunter Energy Monitor, although similar thermostats are available from Honeywell, Johnson Controls, and other companies. These thermostats are inexpensive — as little as $30 — and they plug directly into a wall outlet. You simply plug the refrigerator into the thermostat and insert a temperature probe into the refrigerator. Other models may require wiring an extension cord (or the refrigerator's power cord) to the controller. The illustration on page 133 shows a thermostat that can be used for keeping a refrigerator or freezer at fermentation temperatures.

Thermostats that have an outlet into which you plug the refrigerator are the easiest way to go. However, thermostats that need to be wired to the refrigerator's power cord are not very difficult to install. Such a procedure should take no more than 15 minutes. (Get an extension cord, wire it to the thermostat, and then plug the refrigerator into the extension cord.) The sensing element on these thermostats is usually attached to the thermostat by a thin wire that easily slips under the door gasket and into the refrigerator.

KEEPING THE FERMENTER WARM

Although most homebrewers seem to worry most about keeping the fermenter cool during warm weather, a number of homebrewers also worry about how to keep the fermenter from getting too cold. If the fermenter temperature becomes too low, the yeast may stop working altogether, giving you a stuck fermentation.

Some ways to keep the fermenter warm include: light bulbs, insulated area, room heater, electric towel heaters, and pipe tape. If you use any of these, please be safety conscious — *avoid having combustible material near exposed heating elements, avoid putting heat sources in places where small hands could reach them, avoid any exposed electrical wires, and generally just use common sense.*

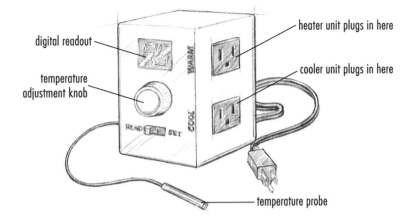

digital readout

temperature
adjustment knob

heater unit plugs in here

cooler unit plugs in here

temperature probe

*Fermenters can require heating and cooling, and a **thermostatic
controller** like this one can control the sources of both.*

In addition to the heat source, you'll need some kind of thermostatic controller to turn it off and on. Brewers Resource sells a
nifty controller that can control both a heat source and a cooling
source. This unit can be tied to a 100-watt incandescent bulb
mounted inside a refrigerator or freezer, as well as the refrigerator's
compressor. If the temperature gets too warm, it turns on the compressor. If it gets too cold, it turns on the light bulb. This is our
favorite approach because consistency is ensured. The problem
with just controlling the refrigerator is that if the ambient temperature becomes too cold (usually not a problem in a house
with central heating), no heat source is available to maintain a
constant environment. A similar controller, available at lower
cost, is made by Johnson Controls (model A-19).

One very nice way to keep a fermenter warm in a too-cold
environment is to use an aquarium heater (or similar immersion-
type heating element). To do this, put the carboy in a large plastic trash can or a large bucket (the Rubbermaid bucket that we
recommend for soaking bottles will also work well for this).
Fill the trash can with water, insert the aquarium heater, and
you're all set.

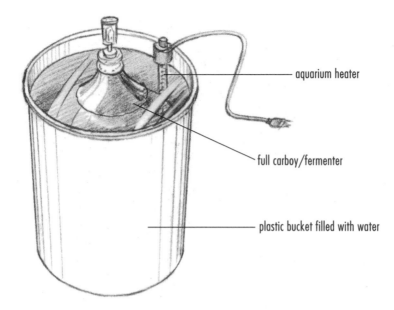

aquarium heater

full carboy/fermenter

plastic bucket filled with water

*An **aquarium heater** is a neat way to keep a fermenter warm. Just put the fermenter in a large plastic bucket, drop in the heater, and you're set.*

If you want to get really elaborate and you have a high gadgetude quotient, try building a special fermenter room. This doesn't need to be a very large area. Look to the wine aficionado crowd for some ideas on how to do this. Wine-makers have been building wine cellars at ale fermentation temperatures for years. These make great fermentation rooms and can be built fairly inexpensively. You can even buy them prebuilt for about $1,000. (Call the Wine Enthusiast for a catalog.)

The fermenter room works best in an area that is generally cool (such as a cellar) but not so cold that it needs to be heated. If that happens, you'll need to incorporate both a heating and a cooling source. To build a fermenter room, you need a small area that can be very well insulated. This can be done using several layers of rigid building insulation and an air-conditioner controlled by a Hunter Airstat. You must use an air-conditioner that has a closed vent. You want to recycle the air in the room, cooling it and keeping the heat on the outside of the room.

Remember that an air-conditioner is a heat exchanger, and not an overly efficient one. You are putting energy into the unit while you're also pulling heat from the fermenter room. There will be a buildup of heat in the basement unless it is a rather large space, vented well, or you can plan for some means of exhausting the heat outdoors. If not, you are going to have a problem as the heat builds up around the fermenter room. The higher the ambient

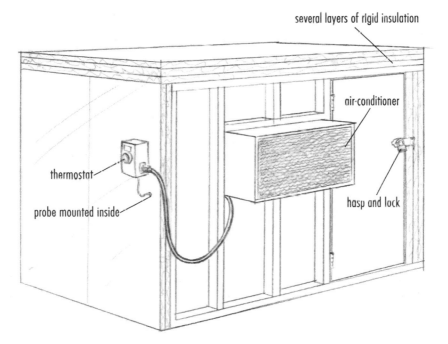

*If you've got the space, time, and money, you might consider building an **insulated fermenter room** in your cellar or garage. (Note: Front insulation is not shown in illustration in order to show detail.)*

temperature around the fermenter room, the more cooling will be required. The more the air-conditioner runs, the higher the ambient temperature. You get the idea. With that in mind, see the illustration on page 137 for a simple fermenter room that can be kept plenty cool for ales, wines, ciders, and so on. (Lagers need a different approach.)

We're not going to recommend any specific size or details, but it is best to plan on the outside dimensions being multiples of 2 or 4 feet. Rigid insulation comes in 4 foot by 8 foot sheets, and that way you can minimize wasted material. The frame is made entirely of 2 x 4s and set on 16-inch centers. You can fill the area between the studs with fiberglass insulation. The door is a simple 2 x 4 frame with half-lap joints for added strength and filled with rigid insulation. Standard weather stripping should be used around the door and frame to seal it. A good-quality tape such as that used on vapor barriers should be used to seal all edges and cracks.

Light Protection

Some homebrewers forget that light can affect fermenting wort. Most homebrewers are familiar with the skunky aroma of lightstruck beer from clear or green bottles; but many forget that light reacts with isomerized hops, and hops are isomerized in the boil.

If you use plastic buckets, brew kettles, or stainless-steel kegs as your fermenters, you don't have to worry about light — only brewers fermenting in glass need to block light. A carboy sitting in a sunny room (or one with fluorescent lighting) for a week is going to develop the same skunky compounds that you find in beers sold in clear or green bottles. There are several ways to protect your beer from light damage.

Trash bag. Use a large, dark-colored "lawn and leaf" plastic trash bag to cover your carboy. Poke a hole in the top for the airlock or blow-off tube, or simply tie it shut around the carboy neck.

Carboy box. New carboys usually come in large cardboard boxes that are, obviously, just the right size for the carboy. Cut a hole in the top for the airlock or blow-off tube, and you're in business.

Closet. As always, the lowest gadgetude approach is often the best. If you've got a closet, basement, pantry, or similar space, use it. Just be sure to avoid a pantry or walk-in closet fitted with fluorescent lighting.

Bedsheet. Drape an old bedsheet or towel over the carboy. You can also simply wrap it around the neck and tie it securely in place while allowing a blow-off tube or airlock to be exposed.

FERMENTING VESSELS

Most of the basic homebrewing equipment sets sold in the United States today are based on a plastic bucket fermenter. If you are a frugal beginner who doesn't want to buy a beginning equipment kit, the fermenter is easy enough to make.

Plastic Buckets

Many homebrewers started out in the hobby with a simple 5- to 7-gallon plastic bucket as their fermenter. To make a similar unit, you will need to find a large, food-grade plastic bucket. Donut shops are a good place to try (jelly filling is often shipped in plastic buckets), as are fast-food restaurants (pickles often come in plastic buckets, but it's hard to get rid of the aroma). Many places will give the buckets to you if you ask. Plastics companies may have several different choices.

Once you have the bucket, you need a rubber grommet (a dollar can get you four). Buy a grommet with a ⅜-inch-diameter inside hole to fit the airlock. Drill a ½-inch-diameter hole in the center of the lid, and fit the hole with the rubber grommet. That's it. You've got a plastic fermenter. You'll now need an airlock. You can either buy one for about $1 at a homebrew supply store, or see airlocks and blow-off tubes on pages 125 to 127.

Pots

Stainless-steel or enamel brewing pots also can be used as fermenters. If you are using an open fermentation system, the pot is ideal. It is large enough for a 5-gallon batch, has a lid if you want to close the top to airborne contaminants until the kraeusen kicks up, and is easily cleaned. In descriptions of his EasyMasher system, Jack Schmidling advocates using the mash kettle as a fermentation vessel. There is no reason this won't work. Although some homebrewers are uneasy about using pots as fermenters because they prefer closed systems over open systems, many award-winning homebrewers have had great success using kettles as fermenters.

Carboys

Probably the single most popular approach to fermentation vessels (at least among people who've been involved in the hobby for a while) is the glass carboy. These are inexpensive, very durable, easy to keep clean and sanitary, and easy to adapt for the sealed-fermentation approach favored by most brewers. The ideal size is about 6½ to 7 gallons, although 5 gallons are adequate for most uses. Combined with devices such as the BrewCap or Fermentap, the carboy essentially duplicates the function of a cylindroconical fermenter. Although carboys are available at almost every homebrew supply shop, you can sometimes find them for only the cost of a deposit from bottled-water companies. (Most bottled-water companies today are abandoning glass carboys in favor of lighter, less breakable, plastic carboys.) Other good sources of glass carboys are glass or pottery outlets. Mark bought most of his 5-gallon carboys from a Corning Revere Outlet in Martinsburg, West Virginia, for $10 to $11 each. There are many Corning outlets around the country, so check your Yellow Pages or look for large factory outlet centers. (Corning outlets are also good places to look for stainless-steel kettles, stainless-steel stirring spoons, and yard ale glasses.)

Karl went to one bottled-water supplier in Missouri and simply asked, "How much for a used carboy?" Glass ones cost him about $10; plastic cost $7.00. Prices may vary at other sources.

Because plastic carboys are becoming the preferred distribution vessel for bottled water, homebrewers have experimented with them as fermenters. Plastic carboys are very inexpensive, easily obtained, easy to work with, and hard to break. Unfortunately they are easily scratched and difficult to sanitize over the long term. Some homebrewers are also concerned that the plastic is permeable to oxygen and that, because the bottles are stamped "safe for water only," they may not be tolerant of alcohol-containing liquids or those that are acidic. Checking the bottom of a few plastic carboys for the plastic identifier number told us nothing, as they were all labeled "7 — Other." This is not acceptable to us. Why use a mystery material that could ruin your beer? If you want to try fermenting with plastic carboys, you probably should cycle through them, never using one for more than a batch or two before returning it to the bottled water company. Again, we have heard of people using them repeatedly with no problems. We've also heard of people using plastic trash cans, but we don't recommend that either.

Using Carboys

Carboys are always used as closed-fermentation systems (at least we've never heard of anyone trying to do an open fermentation in a carboy). The beer is siphoned in through the neck with a siphon hose, the yeast is pitched, and the carboy is sealed, usually with a plastic carboy cap that fits snugly over the top and has two holes for blow-off tubes or airlocks. If you'd rather, you can seal the carboy with a rubber stopper (#6½ or #7) that has a hole drilled for an airlock.

EMPTYING A CARBOY

When you clean a carboy, you'll often fill it most of the way with water or a chlorine bleach solution. Emptying the carboy can be difficult because the liquid glugs out of the bottle. This can be avoided by simply inserting a racking tube up the neck of the bottle as you empty it, thereby breaking the airlock. Presto! Smooth, quick flow.

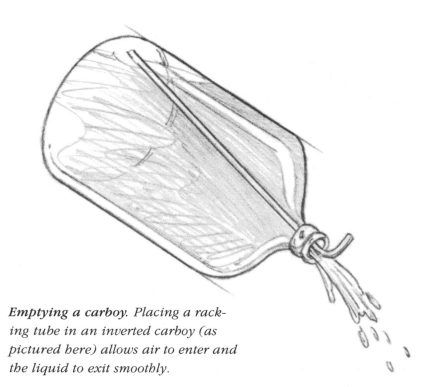

Emptying a carboy. Placing a racking tube in an inverted carboy (as pictured here) allows air to enter and the liquid to exit smoothly.

To empty the carboy, use a siphon tube again, this time gently moving it from the fermenter to a priming vessel for bottling, or to a secondary fermenter or keg.

If you have a kegging setup, you don't need to worry about siphoning the liquid from the carboy. You can do the transfer in a closed manner simply by (1) running a racking tube through one hole in the rubber carboy cap almost to the bottom of the carboy, and (2) inserting a hose from a CO_2 tank into the other hole. You then attach a hose from the racking tube to a similar racking tube on the second carboy. Because the racking tube on this carboy also extends almost to the bottom, the transfer will be done gently without splashing. Then, as you hold down the rubber carboy cap on the vessel containing your beer, CO_2 pressure will force the liquid to move from one carboy to the other, avoiding worries about how to start the siphon or breaking the vacuum. Don't use clamps on the carboy cap because too much pressure build-up can shatter the glass.

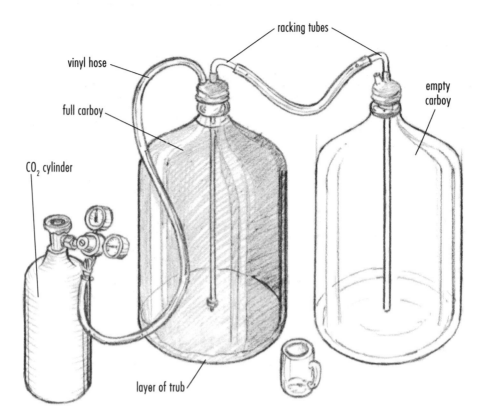

racking tubes

vinyl hose

empty carboy

full carboy

CO_2 cylinder

layer of trub

If you have a kegging setup, there is no need to siphon beer from your carboy. Use your CO_2 cylinder and a racking configuration like this

After the beer has been removed, there is usually a layer of sticky, brownish goo clinging to the shoulders of the carboy. This is especially true after a primary fermentation. An easy way to remove this is to add 2 gallons of water and a couple ounces of bleach. Place a solid stopper in the mouth and turn the carboy upside down. Set the carboy in a bucket or a milk crate and go do something else. In a few days, the layer of crud will be loosened and may just rinse free. You might have to scrub it out with a carboy brush in any case, but this procedure will make the job easier.

Glass carboys are breakable. If you shake or rock them to aerate the wort prior to pitching, be careful not to hit objects that could crack the glass. Many homebrewers break carboys while trying to siphon the hot wort directly into the carboy without using a chiller. Carboys do not withstand thermal stress and are not intended for handling hot liquids. Nor are they intended to be used as pressure vessels. Do not apply pressure to them when no relief mechanism is available.

Moving Carboys

A gallon of water weighs more than 8 pounds. Multiply that by 5 gallons, add the weight of the carboy, and consider that wort is more dense than water, and you're talking about lugging 50 pounds around in the form of a fragile glass vessel. This is something we worry about.

The most popular way to move a carboy is with a plastic-encased metal handle that goes around the neck (see the illustration below). These are available from some homebrew supply stores. They seem to work well for carrying empty carboys, but we don't trust them with the added weight of more than 40 pounds of precious, unfermented beer.

A better approach is to use something that supports the weight of the carboy from the bottom. Plastic milk crates work fine. Don't steal these from the loading dock of your local convenience store;

*A plastic-encased metal **carboy handle** will make your life much easier.*

they're easy enough to find in most department stores or home improvement centers, and they're inexpensive. We managed to get some at a Kmart for less than $5 each.

We think the best way to move carboys is with rolling carboy carriers. We first saw these used in 1989 by a member of the Chesapeake Real Ale Brewers (CRAB), and we've yet to see a better solution. You basically construct a platform with a lip to keep the carboy in place and then put caster wheels on the bottom so that it can be rolled from the brewery area to the fermenter area. This doesn't solve the problem of moving a carboy up or down stairs, but if you brew and ferment on the same level, it's a real back-saver. The illustration on page 146 shows how to make this great little device.

One neat improvement that can save some backaches is to add a handle or tow rope. Cut about a 6-foot length and tie it (you may want to drill holes for the rope) to two corners — like the rope on a sled.

Materials for a Rolling Carboy Carrier

One 13"x13" platform of ¾" plywood
Four 1"-wide x 12"-long strips of ¾" plywood
Four swivel casters
Sixteen #10 ¾"-long wood screws

Directions

1. Cut out the platform and strips from a ¾" plywood sheet.
2. Glue and clamp the strips to the platform in the pattern illustrated.
3. Attach the swivel casters with the wood screws 1" in from the edges (be sure to drill pilot holes first).
4. Set the carboy on the platform, fill, attach airlock, and roll into the fermenter closet or corner.

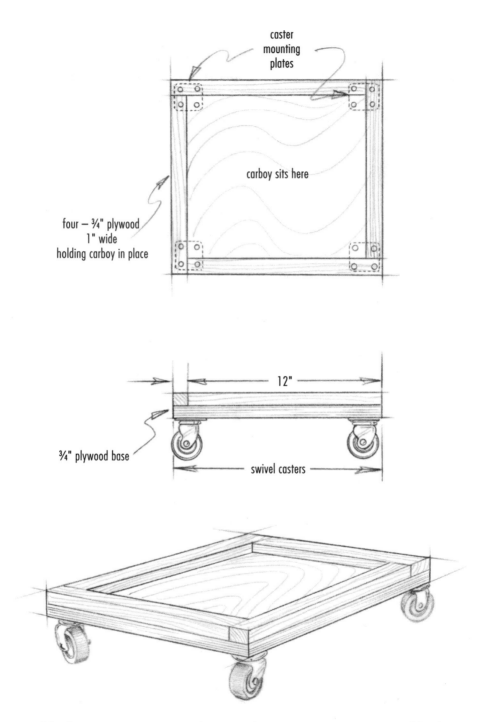

caster mounting plates

carboy sits here

four — ¾" plywood 1" wide holding carboy in place

12"

¾" plywood base

swivel casters

*The best way to move a carboy is with a **rolling carboy carrier** like this.*

Inverted Carboys:
The BrewCap Method

Several years ago, Kinney Baughman of BrewCo in Boone, North Carolina, began marketing a capping device that was intended to be used with the carboy upside down in a stand. It was called the BrewCap, and it had two hoses going through it: a long tube extending to the top of the inverted carboy, and a short tube extending only into the neck. The long tube is used as a pressure-relief mechanism, and the short tube is used to remove expended yeast and trub that settle into the mouth of the carboy.

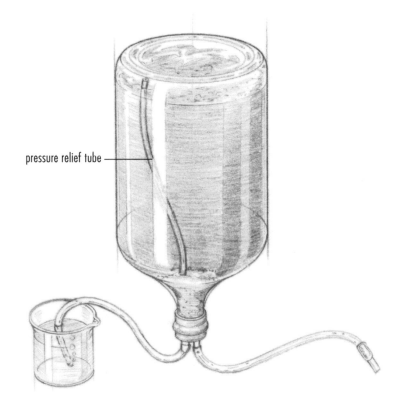

pressure relief tube

*The **BrewCap device** eliminates racking to a secondary fermenter, allows yeast harvesting, and uses gravity to transfer beer to a priming vessel. The short tube (lower right) is used to remove expended yeast and trub that settles into the mouth of the carboy.*

In practice, however, trub often settles on the shoulders of the carboy, and you will need to twist the carboy sharply once or twice a day to loosen this matter and let it fall into the carboy mouth.

The advantages of the BrewCap system are that it:

✔ Eliminates racking to a secondary fermenter. You get the advantages of a secondary ferment, namely, removal of trub from the clean beer without having to siphon the wort to another fermenter.

✔ Allows yeast harvesting. If you want to repitch or culture yeast from settled yeast, you can easily remove yeast from the fermenter.

✔ Eliminates siphoning finished beer. When fermentation is complete, you can simply open the bottom hose and let the beer flow into a priming vessel.

✔ Is totally closed. There is no opportunity for airborne contamination.

The Fermentap, which came on the market in 1994, is similar to the BrewCap. This system works in the same way as the BrewCap, but it includes a solidly built stand that supports the inverted carboy. The BrewCap retails for about $14; the Fermentap for about $30.

*The **Fermentap**, which is similar to the BrewCap system, comes with its own stand.*

There is one area of concern with an inverted carboy system, though. Because the system is upside down and the cap is sealed tight, the fermenter becomes potentially explosive if the hoses get clogged. We have never heard of clogged tubes causing carboys to burst with these setups, but it's not impossible; we urge homebrewers who use this system to keep an eye on vigorous fermentations. It is also impractical to dry hop a beer using a BrewCap. The BrewCap is ideally suited to an area with constant temperature. The instructions recommend not putting it in a refrigerator, which would be difficult to do in any case.

When you buy a BrewCap from BrewCo, you need to supply your own carboy and your own stand. The stands are easy to build; the easiest way to do it is with two milk crates. Saw a

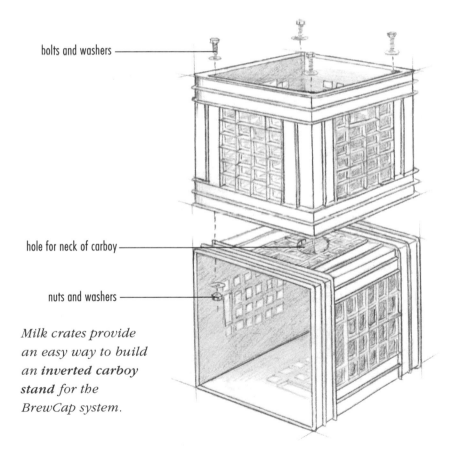

bolts and washers

hole for neck of carboy

nuts and washers

Milk crates provide an easy way to build an inverted carboy stand for the BrewCap system.

hole in the bottom of one so that the inverted carboy can be set down into the crate with the neck through the hole. The second crate will support the upper crate and allow you room to work. Set the crate on end with the opening facing you, and then cut a large square hole in the top to accommodate the carboy neck and hoses. Fasten the two crates together using bolts and washers.

As we mentioned before, a stand is not necessary with the Fermentap because that product comes with its own stand.

AERATING THE WORT

Vigorously healthy yeast growth is possible only if there is adequate oxygen in the wort. Most homebrewers get the needed oxygen into the wort by splashing the beer into the fermenter, shaking the fermenter, or going through various combinations of shaking and rocking the vessel to cause splashing. Some people use pumps to introduce air into the wort. A few homebrewers bubble pure oxygen into the wort through a diffusion stone. Although it is theoretically possible to over-oxygenate the wort with this method, it is impossible for a homebrewer using rocking or shaking techniques to overaerate the wort. Rocking produces enough oxygen for healthy yeast growth (though still at levels well below ideal).

Two methods we like for aerating wort are the use of an aeration hose and the simple rocking of carboys to encourage splashing.

The aeration hose is essentially a tube that fits on the end of a siphon hose. It is usually made of copper tubing with many holes drilled in the last 6 inches or so, and sealed with an end-cap, which forces the wort to splash through the holes. (There is evidence that leaving the end open, rather than sealed, may actually be more effective.) To make one, get a short length of copper tubing with an outer diameter equal to the inner diameter of your siphon hose. Using a very small drill bit (1/16 inch), drill a series of holes about ½ inch apart throughout the length of the pipe, as shown in the illustration here. Affix an end-cap to the end of the tube and solder into place (remember to avoid solders with lead content).

In an article in the March/April 1995 issue of *Brewing Techniques,* Richard Humbert described how to build a cradle for rocking a carboy. The idea is simple and effective; it is a neat gadget that we're surprised others haven't been building for years. Basically, you build a box cradle, or rack, for your carboy to rest in, get a sealed cap without holes to keep the wort in the carboy (rubber stoppers work well), and put rockers on the cradle so that it rocks back and forth like a rocking chair, shaking the fermenter. Humbert emphasizes the need for a gentle radius to give the unit stability. He rocks the unit vigorously for about five minutes.

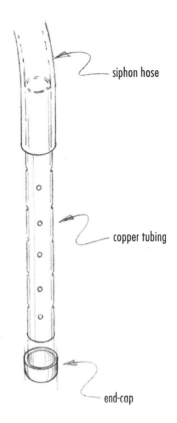

*A simple **aeration hose** such as this one allows air to get into the wort to promote vigorous yeast growth.*

If you are really worried about aerating your wort and you love gadgets, an air pump can be used to introduce air into the wort. Be sure to filter the air so that only clean air goes into the fermenter. Simply building a chamber and filling it with cotton should work fine for the air filter, although one homebrewer we know says you should also spray the cotton with grain alcohol solution. If you don't already have a pump and you want to try this method, Brewers Resource sells an aeration kit that includes the pump, filter, and a diffusion stone. If you're a super beer geek

siphon hose

copper tubing

end-cap

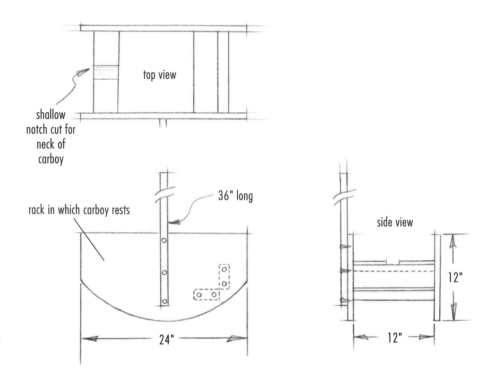

top view

shallow notch cut for neck of carboy

rack in which carboy rests

36" long

side view

24"

12"

12"

*A **wort rocker** for your carboy is one of those devices people should have been making a long time ago.*

with an enormous gadgetude quotient, then you can also get a splitter that will let you simultaneously aerate two or even three carboys with a single pump. This could be useful if you're doing 10- or 15-gallon batches and then fermenting them in two or three carboys.

If you prefer to elevate the wort oxygen levels by bubbling pure oxygen into the wort rather than by aerating it, buy a new (don't buy used) tank, a regulator made for oxygen, and a diffusion stone. A setup consisting of a small oxygen tank with a suitable valve and diffusion stone should cost around $35. Although we prefer to aerate our wort, the bubbling approach is a fairly inexpensive way to experiment with pure oxygen, and you may find this approach to work well for you.

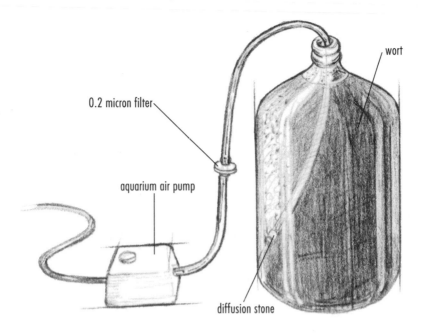

wort

0.2 micron filter

aquarium air pump

diffusion stone

*If you are really concerned that your yeast is oxygen-starved, you might try aerating your wort with an **air pump**. One intended for an aquarium will work fine.*

CORNELIUS KEGS

The Cornelius keg is a great way to store finished beer, but it's difficult to use as a fermenter. (Well, it's difficult to use for a primary fermenter, anyway.) The problem with the Cornelius keg is that a vigorous fermentation can easily clog the valves. If you want to use a Cornelius keg as a fermenter, first take a wrench and remove the *In* or gas valve. This will give a ⅜-inch opening for a blow-off tube or airlock. It is a small opening, however, that can easily clog during primary fermentation, letting pressure build up inside. This can be extremely dangerous, even though a Cornelius keg can withstand over 100 psi internally. Some homebrewers do use Cornelius kegs in this way, but most stress that they work best if the wort is filtered first.

A Cornelius keg does make an excellent secondary fermenter. You may want to do your primary fermentation in glass, then rack to a Cornelius as a secondary. If you wish to lager, just pop the whole thing in the refrigerator. There are homebrewers who ferment in soda kegs by carefully removing as much trub from the boil as possible, siphoning through the wort chiller (and often a filter) to the soda keg, and attaching a blow-off tube to the top of the keg.

If you use Cornelius kegs as fermenters, you can rack the beer under pressure so that the beer is never exposed to air. You can also naturally carbonate the beer. Wait until the beer approaches terminal gravity, then remove the blow-off tube and replace the gas valve. Finally, pressurize the keg from your CO_2 tank to about 10 psi. Incidentally, soda kegs require some initial pressure to seal properly.

OTHER STAINLESS-STEEL KEGS

Homebrewers love the small 5-gallon Cornelius soda kegs, but many overlook another keg that is the perfect size for homebrewing — the quarter-barrel or pony keg (7.75 U.S. gallons). These are widely available and can be used as fermenters as well as for kegging for your beer (see Chapter 10, Kegging). Pico-Brewing Systems sells half-barrel kegs that are modified for use as fermenters. At $69, this strikes us as the best approach for homebrewers interested in fermenting in stainless steel; however, they may be difficult to clean without caustics. They are recommended for use as secondary fermenters.

STAINLESS-STEEL CYLINDROCONICAL FERMENTERS

Most microbreweries ferment beer in large (15- or 30-barrel) stainless-steel tanks that are in the shape of tall cylinders with a cone at the bottom. Yeast and other matter can settle into the cone and be drained off, which makes this an excellent design for a larger professional brewery. For small-scale use, the equipment becomes prohibitively expensive. But if you have a lot of cash, you can purchase a stainless-steel cylindroconical fermenter. These come in sizes as small as 5 gallons (although these smaller sizes are extremely difficult to find), but half-barrel size is more common (Brewers Warehouse has one of the nicest we've seen).

The half-barrel cylindroconical fermenter sold by Brewers Warehouse is made of type 304 stainless steel and has a capacity of 20 gallons. It provides a thermostat to control temperature and a chill band through which you can circulate either cold water or glycol to cool the tank. A pump for the coolant is available at extra cost. Before you start drooling, you should be aware that these fermenters start at about $1,900. If you're very serious about the hobby, these are outrageously cool toys; but for those of us with more proletarian budgets, the inverted carboys discussed earlier have a lot of merit. It is also possible to find cylindroconical plastic vessels of sizes appropriate to homebrewing. U.S. Plastics is one source of these vessels.

Fermenter Shape

One other aspect of fermenters that we'll mention in passing is their geometry. About 50 years ago, Jean deClerck, in discussing the ideal shape and size of brewery fermenters, said to avoid slim, tall cylinders with relatively little surface area (like a Cornelius keg). For practical homebrewing purposes, we see little merit in debating the geometry of fermenters, but the geometry of carboys as fermenters fits in fairly well with deClerck's optimal configurations. Many commercial breweries also use shallow, wide, open fermenters with great success, so deClerck's views do not preclude other perfectly workable solutions.

Summary

We recommend that most homebrewers use a glass carboy with a simple blow-off tube or an airlock. There are a lot of complicated gadgets to choose from, but most simply add more complexity and greater cost. For homebrewers working with large batches, the modified barrels from Pico-Brewing Systems make more sense to us than juggling several glass carboys; however, the carboys have the advantage of encouraging experiments with split batches, such as for comparing yeasts. We also like the inverted carboy approach, and many brewers should be tempted by the benefits of this method.

– 9 –

BOTTLING

HOMEBREWERS SEEM TO MOVE ON TO KEGS at some point in their brewing career, but there are still many reasons why bottles make sense, even for the experienced homebrewer who kegs most batches:

- ✔ Not enough refrigerator space for kegs
- ✔ Cost of kegging equipment (usually at least $150)
- ✔ Competitions require bottles
- ✔ Don't like complicated equipment
- ✔ Don't consume beer often enough to drink a keg
- ✔ Still testing the waters (rather, beers) to see if the hobby is right
- ✔ Like to keep samples of past batches for aging

CHOOSING BOTTLES

There are several kinds of bottles used by homebrewers:

- ✔ 7-ounce pony bottles
- ✔ 12-ounce brown bar bottles

✔ 16-ounce brown bar bottles
✔ 20-ounce swing-top Grolsch bottles
✔ 22-ounce brown bottles
✔ 25-ounce bottles
✔ 1-liter champagne bottles
✔ 2-liter plastic bottles

Avoid using bottles that are not designed for carbonated beverages — they cannot withstand the pressure and can shatter easily, creating a dangerous situation and also wasting the beer you've taken such care to make.

Most homebrewers use the 12-ounce longneck brown bottles; the strongest of these are known as "bar bottles" or "returnable bottles," although returnable bottles are becoming increasingly harder to find. The advantage of the 12-ounce bottle is that it's easy to find, looks the way people think a beer bottle should look, is just the right size for one serving of most types of beer, and can be entered in competitions. Conventional wisdom is that you should avoid twist-off type bottles because they can't be capped or because they don't hold a seal well. We've found, though, that most cappers will put a cap on these bottles. So, if you're satisfied with the seal, there's no reason to avoid twist-off bottles. However, we still don't trust them for laying-down beers that we will be keeping for more than several months.

Larger-size bottles — that is, bigger than the 12-ounce size — are attractive in that washing, filling, and capping bottles is a chore and most people would like to minimize their workload. The following table compares the number of bottles you would need for a 5-gallon batch for each of several types of commonly used bottles. Although using large bottles is generally a good idea, keep in mind that each one may hold more beer than you want to drink at one sitting; moreover, if you enter competitions, you may find that most large bottles will be declared ineligible.

NUMBER OF BOTTLES NEEDED FOR 5 GALLONS OF HOMEBREW

Bottle Size (ounces)	Number Needed
7	92
12	54
16	40
20	32
22	29
25	26
67.6 (2 liters)	10

For high-gravity brews, such as barleywine, dopplebock, or mead, smaller bottles are often a better choice because few people want to drink a full glass of a thick, syrupy elixir. Most small bottles are twist-offs, and although there has been quite a bit of discussion in homebrewing literature about avoiding twist-offs, we find that they actually do seal acceptably well. Our advice is to try a couple of these bottles with your next batch and see if you have problems with their ability to hold a seal.

The Grolsch swing-top bottles are great for beer, but they are usually ineligible for use in competitions. For everyday use, this is one of our favorite bottles: They are large, easy to clean, easy to seal (just swing the top down and clamp it), and look really cool. The rubber seals do wear out over time, and you'll need to replace the gaskets every few batches. Most homebrew supply shops do stock them, however, and replacing them is a simple task.

The plastic 2-liter PET (polyethylene terephthalate) bottles, commonly used for soda and wine coolers, are a good choice for bottling beer. These also come in other sizes, but 2-liter is the most common. They will not stand up to scrubbing and cannot be run through dishwashers, so sanitizing them presents some challenges; but if the bottles are rinsed well when first empty, they can easily be sanitized with chlorine, iodophor, or other popular sanitizing solutions. The plastic bottles are also a good choice if you're planning on bringing homebrew to a picnic, beach party, or other outdoor event where you may not want to worry about glass breakage. There is also no need to bother with a bottle capper — simply screw the twist-top back on.

There are some disadvantages to PET bottles, however. They are large — more than even most dedicated beer drinkers would want to consume at one time. Resealing partially empty bottles will keep the carbonation for a little while, but eventually the beer will go flat. These bottles are also somewhat permeable to oxygen and may, over time, lose CO_2 or become oxidized. The bottles admit light, so you need to store them in a dark place to prevent skunking. Also, the cap seals wear out and are not readily replaceable. This may not be a problem, though, because the bottles also may scratch over time, and you're better off discarding the bottles after a couple of uses. If your family drinks a lot of soda, you have a ready supply of replacement bottles.

The Color of Bottles

Some homebrewers believe that the color of beer bottles is purely a matter of aesthetics and personal choice. Hogwash. Beer is sensitive to light in the range of 450 to 520 nanometers (nm), which means that exposing beer to sunlight or fluorescent light will cause an unpleasant skunky smell and flavor. Clear bottles offer no protection against this. Green bottles offer very little protection. Brown bottles afford fairly good protection (but still should not be relied on completely to prevent skunking).

All homebrewers would do well to keep their beer out of the light. Because most brewers keep the bottles in boxes in a closet or in a refrigerator, there's very little chance for light exposure; and if you're careful about this, you can even get away with using clear or green bottles. But given the amount of time and energy you put into brewing, you won't want to take chance of ruining your beer by mishandling it.

Finding Bottles

Looking for bottles? Finding bottles should be one of the easiest tasks facing a homebrewer. After all, you've probably been drinking various commercial beer for years, and good beers are usually sold in bottles that are suitable for homebrewer uses. You could try asking a few friends who don't make their own beer to save their empties for you if you're not building up your own supply quickly enough.

One of the best ways to obtain good, usable bottles is to visit a bar or restaurant and get to know the bartenders or wait staff. If the place serves Grolsch or similar beer in swing top bottles, you're really in luck. Restaurants that have Sunday champagne brunches are also a good resource because they have a constant supply of large bottles. This is where the offer of trading some of your homebrew for a few bottles can work wonders.

You could also try going through the dumpsters behind bars to find bottles, although these are often filthy and need to be washed well. Recycling centers are also a good place to look. In one local area, the recyclers will not give brewers most beer bottles but they *will* give up their Grolsch bottles because their equipment is incapable of handling the ceramic top and wire enlosure. Incredibly, they usually just send them to the local landfill.

If you want to use the large Grolsch bottles and cannot find them at a local bar, you can probably buy them from your local homebrew supply shop. Grolsch bottles are sold by E-Z Cap of Calgary, Alberta, and are available to homebrewers through homebrew supply shops. Many of the homebrew supply shops also sell the regular 12-ounce beer bottles, but why buy what's easily obtained for free?

Choosing Caps

Most homebrewers use ordinary crown caps for bottling. These are not very expensive at all and are readily available at homebrew shops. Some homebrew suppliers also have soda overrun caps in stock. When you can find them, you can usually buy an incredible amount of caps at an unbelievably low price. If you don't care about spending money but would rather have the "best," look for oxygen-absorbing bottle caps. These can reduce the risk of your bottled beer oxidizing and developing off flavors in the bottle.

CLEANING BOTTLES

One of the most labor intensive, and least popular, parts of the homebrewing hobby is cleaning bottles. When you first get bottles, they often have mold inside and labels attached. The easiest way to get the labels off is to soak them for several days in a tub of ammonia solution. Rubbermaid makes a very large plastic tub that works well for soaking bottles. You could also try soaking them in chlorine bleach solution, but we have not found this method especially effective for removing the labels, although it does loosen mold quite well. Never mix ammonia with chlorine bleach — these are separate, independent approaches to bottle cleaning. Finally, a trash can with a lid also works well for soaking. It keeps the odors from offending your family and neighbors.

CAUTION

Never mix chlorine and ammonia — the fumes can be deadly.

After soaking them, you may need to scrub the bottles. All homebrew supply shops sell brushes that reach into bottles, but an alternative approach is to use water pressure to clean the bottles.

The Bottle Washer

Several companies market bottle washers that work by spraying water into the bottle. These usually come with garden hose threads, which work well for most faucets on laundry tubs, but you'll need to buy a separate adapter for use with a kitchen sink (you may already have the adapter if you've had to attach a wort chiller to a kitchen faucet). These adapters also can be found at many plumbing-supply and hardware stores.

Bottle washers are U-shaped and usually made of brass. They are tough, durable, inexpensive, and effective. Three that we're aware of are made by: JET Carboy & Bottle Washer, Fermenthaus, and Chateau. These work simply by attaching them to the sink, turning on the water, and pressing down on the valve with the bottle to get it to spray. They also work well for cleaning carboys.

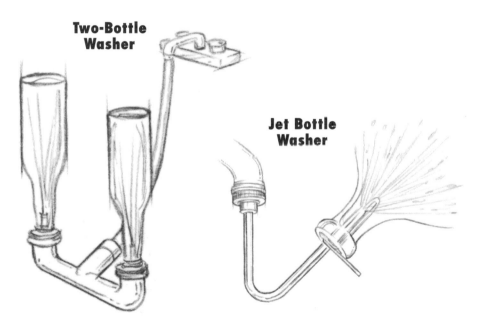

Two-Bottle Washer

Jet Bottle Washer

*The best way to wash bottles is to use a **jet bottle washer**. Better yet, use a jet bottle washer that can handle two bottles at once.*

Prices range from about $8 to $20. Bottle washers are one gadget that we unequivocally recommend. They make cleaning much easier and are so inexpensive that there's no reason not to own one. For those concerned about water usage, bottle washers are a downright "must-have" item. When you are ready to wash or rinse a bottle all you need to do is get ready to run water.

One bottle washer that stands out from the rest of the products mentioned here is the Double Blast bottle washer from Fermtech. It has two jets. This lets you clean two bottles at once, thereby reducing the amount of time you spend washing. It sells for about $14; as with other bottle washers, it works fine with a laundry tub faucet, but you'll need an adapter to use it on a kitchen sink.

The Bottle Tree

The bottle tree is a plastic rack for drying and storing cleaned bottles. It consists of a column with knobs pointed upward on which you hang the bottles to dry. These are available from various sources; one of the nicer units we've seen is available through Williams Brewing of San Leandro, California (see Suppliers). Their tree includes a sterilant sprayer that works as follows: You fill the tray with a sterilant solution, such as chlorine bleach or iodophor, then push the bottle down over a nozzle, which activates a little pump that squirts sterilant into the bottle. You then hang the bottle on the knobs to dry.

If you want to build your own bottle tree, you can do so easily by using an untreated 4" x 4" piece of wood as your column and building a base from lengths of 2" x 4" lumber. The pegs to hold the bottles can be made easily from a ½-inch hardwood dowel. This approach probably will not save you any money, but it will be more durable than a plastic bottle tree and is fun to make.

Materials for a Bottle Tree

One 4x4 at least 40" long (but
you can round it up to 48"
and add more pegs).
Forty-eight pegs, 3" long, made
from ½"-hardwood dowel
(12' of dowel required)
Two 28"-long 2x4s
One ⅜" x 4"-long lag screw
Washer for lag screw

Tools

Electric drill
Drilling jig
⅜" spade bit

Directions

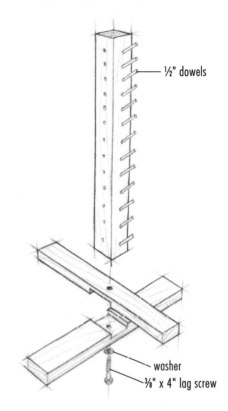

½" dowels

washer
⅜" x 4" lag screw

*A homemade bottle tree is
easy to make and well worth
the effort.*

1. Cut a dado ¾" deep by 3½"
   wide in the center of both
   2x4s. You are making a half
   lap joint, so take your time
   and trim as necessary.
2. Cut your pegs from the dowels.
3. Starting 3" from the base and in the middle of the 4x4,
   mark a point every 3" for the ½"-diameter holes. Do this
   for all four sides.
4. Using a drilling jig set at 60°, drill a 1"-deep hole at every
   mark.
5. Glue the pegs into the holes.
6. Assemble the legs and drill a ⅜"-diameter hole through
   the center point of the crossover. Glue and clamp the
   two leg pieces and let dry.

7. Drill a countersink hole ¾" by ⅜" deep in the center of the crossover. Then drill a ⅜" hole all the way through the center of the crossover.

8. Drill a ¼"-diameter hole 2½" deep into the bottom center of the 4x4.

9. Put the washer over the lag screw and insert into the countersink hole. Attach the legs to the base.

10. Finish is optional. (Use either a gloss polyurethane or a high-gloss oil-based paint. It's easier to clean and sanitize.)

Note: A simple drilling jig can be made from a piece of 2"x12" lumber. Cut a 60° slope across the 2x12. Set this on the 4x4 and lay the drill along the sloped side. This works for most drills and takes a bit of practice on some scrap wood to get the hang of it.

Bottle-Sanitation Methods

Three methods are commonly used for sanitizing bottles prior to filling: rinsing with chemical sanitizers, running the bottles through a dishwasher with a heat cycle, and baking the bottles in an oven.

Chemical Sanitizers. Rinsing bottles with chemical sanitizers is the most common, and probably the most effective, way that homebrewers sanitize their bottles. The chemicals used are the same ones used for cleaning surfaces and equipment: chlorine bleach solution, iodophor, trisodium phosphate (TSP), and B-Brite or similar oxidants.

Dishwasher. Dishwashers are a promising way of sanitizing bottles. You can put some sanitizer, such as iodophor, into the dishwasher and run it with a heat-dry cycle. This works best with bottles that are pre-scrubbed or that have been well rinsed regularly to eliminate moldy scum.

Oven. Some homebrewers have experimented with sanitizing their bottles by baking them in an oven at 400°F for an hour or so, then letting them cool before bottling. This method sounds promising, but we do not recommend it because the heat stress may weaken the bottles. Brewers who have used this method tell us that their bottles are more prone to breaking during bottling than are their bottles sanitized with other methods. The evidence is admittedly anecdotal, and we hope to see more rigorous tests that conclusively show whether the bottles are weakened or not, but meanwhile, we're more comfortable recommending the other approaches.

Sanitizing Bottle Caps

When you get a bag or box of bottle caps from the homebrew supply shop, you should not assume they are sterile and ready for use. Instead, rinse the caps with a sanitizing agent (e.g., iodophor) or boil them before using. We prefer rinsing them because the seals are made of a fairly soft plastic, and we'd like to be sure we get a consistently good seal. However, we know of no homebrewers who boil caps who have had significant problems with bottles sealing properly.

BOTTLE FILLERS

You'll need a siphon hose with a racking cane to get the beer out of the priming bucket and into the bottle. It's also possible to drill a hole in a bottling bucket and attach a spigot for filling bottles. We don't recommend this approach because of the difficulty in sanitizing the spigot and the increased likelihood of aerating and oxidizing the beer. (It is awfully easy though.)

Make or get some kind of clip that you can attach to the side of the bucket for holding your racking tube. You'll be concentrating on filling your bottles, so you don't want to have to worry about the end in the priming vessel flopping around or lifting out of the beer.

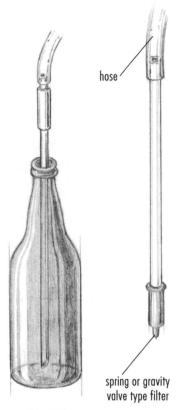

hose

spring or gravity
valve type filter

Phil's Philler

*Bottle fillers can be a
great convenience. The
standard ones use a
spring to control a push
valve on the bottom.
Phil's Philler takes a
different tack. The bottom
is cut at an angle,
allowing beer to flow
smoothly, and flow is
controlled by a push-
valve on top.*

A bottle filler is an attachment to the siphoning hose that lets you control the flow of beer into the bottle with some type of shutoff mechanism. This is typically a push-valve in the bottom of the filler that allows beer to flow when you push down on it and stops the flow when you release the pressure. With most fillers, you fill the bottle up close to the rim, and when you pull the wand out, the volume displaced by the wand itself turns out to give you a good ¾ inch or so of headspace. There are three such products, all somewhat different, that we're aware of: the standard, inexpensive bottle filler with the spring-loaded valve on the tip; the Fermtech filler, which uses a gravity valve without a spring; and the Listermann Phil's Philler, which uses a push-valve at the top of the filler.

Spring-activated plastic bottle fillers are available at most homebrew stores for $2 to $3. Most of these tend to splash the beer into the bottle fairly vigorously. They are known to occasionally stick, causing you to spill a bit of beer, but it's not a big problem. Fermtech improved on the plastic bottle filler by replacing the spring-loaded valve with a gravity-activated one — the valve stays closed unless the tip is pushed into the bottle. One interesting improvement on the basic filler is the Phil's Philler sold by Listermann. This device is made of brass rather than plastic and has no spring at the bottom. Instead, the bottom is cut at an angle and the beer flows smoothly into the bottle. The flow is controlled by a push-valve at the top of the filler rather than the spring-loaded end that is used by other fillers.

Counter-Pressure Bottle Fillers

Only people with kegging systems are likely to be interested in the counter-pressure bottle filler. It lets you store and carbonate your beer in a Cornelius keg and then apply CO_2 pressure to fill a bottle, purging air and nearly eliminating the chance of oxidized aromas and flavors. The counter-pressure bottle filler fills bottles gently and retains the carbonation in the beer.

There are several counter-pressure bottle fillers on the market. Foxx Equipment sells one for $28. Benjamin Machine Products sells one with trigger valves (a nice improvement over the Foxx model) for $59.

There are many other bottle fillers on the market, ranging in price from $30 to $400. One of the more elaborate (and expensive) is the Melvico filler from Vinotheque. This model includes a stand and a plastic shield to protect you from possible glass breakage. An article by David Ruggiero, Jonathan Spillane, and Doug Snyder in the Fall 1995 issue of *Zymurgy* magazine evaluates various counter-pressure bottle fillers and includes test results showing the effectiveness of each in retaining carbonation and purging air. It also discusses the ease of use of each model and the completeness of accompanying instructions. The authors found that the Melvico is one of the easiest to set up and use and one of the best at retaining carbonation. On the less-expensive side of the market, they found that fillers from Braukunst and the Beverage People were effective and fairly easy to use — and cost one-fifth of what the Melvico filler costs.

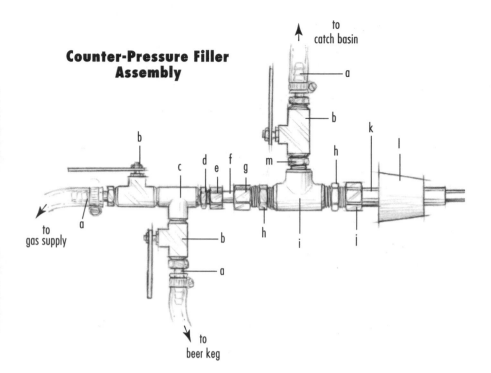

Counter-Pressure Filler Assembly

to catch basin

to gas supply

to beer keg

*A **counter-pressure filler assembly** lets you store beer in a keg, then use CO$_2$ pressure to fill bottles. Note the No. 2 stopper, which you place in the opening of your clean and empty beer bottles.*

a — ¼" MPT x ¼" hose barb

b — ¼" MPT x ¼" FPT on/off valves

c — ¼" FPT Tee

d — ¼" MPT x ¼" comp adapter

e — ¼" compression nut and ferrule (not shown)

f — 18" long ¼" copper or stainless tubing

g — ⅜" compression nut with ⅜ O.D. (outside diameter) O-ring (instead of ferrule)

h — ⅜" comp x ⅜" MPT adapter

i — ⅜" FPT tee

j — ⅜" compression nut with ferrule (not shown)

k — ⅜" copper or stainless tubing, 2" long

l — #2 stopper with ⅜" hole

m — ⅜" MPT x ¼" FPT adapter

It's also possible to build your own counter-pressure filler using parts found readily at many hardware stores. To make the filler, you will need the materials listed below.

Materials for a Counter-Pressure Bottle Filler

Three ¼" MPT x ¼" hose barbs
One ¼" FPT tee
One ⅜" FPT tee
One ¼" MPT x ¼" compression fitting
Two ⅜" MPT x ⅜" compression adapters
Three ¼" MPT x ¼" FPT on-off valves
One ¼" compression nut and ferrule
Two ⅜" compression nuts and ferrule
  (only one ferrule needed)
One ⅜" O.D. (outside diameter) O-ring
One ⅜" MPT x ¼" FPT adapter
One Number 2 drilled rubber stopper
One ⁵⁄₁₆" hose tee for gas line
One 18"-long ¼"-diameter tube (stainless steel,
  brass, or copper)
One 2"-long piece of ⅜"-diameter tube
Teflon tape

Directions

1. Wrap the male connectors with Teflon tape.
2. Assemble according to the diagram on page 172. You'll want the tee for hooking up the CO_2 gas line as shown in the illustration.

To use the counter-pressure bottle filler, first sanitize it with iodophor. Do not use chlorine bleach. Connect everything as shown in the illustration. Insert the filler into a clean bottle. Make sure the stopper seals well, then turn on the gas valve (valve A) to pressurize. Turn off the gas valve A. Turn on the

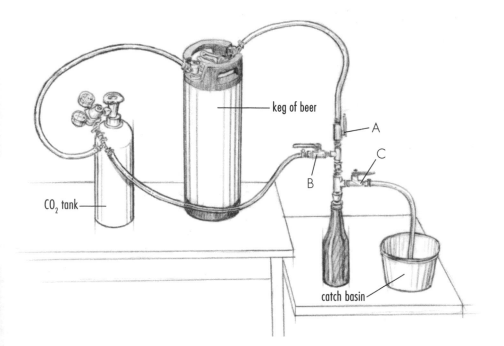

keg of beer

A

C

B

CO₂ tank

catch basin

*To use a **counter-pressure bottle filler**, turn on gas valve (A) to pressurize. Then turn off gas valve, and turn on beer valve (B) and open the bleed valve (C). Gas will escape from the bleed valve and the beer in the keg will be at greater pressure than that of the bottle and will slowly fill it.*

beer valve (valve B). Open the bleed valve (valve C). As the gas escapes from the bleed valve, the beer in the keg will be at greater pressure than that of the bottle and will slowly fill it. When it gets full, close the beer valve (valve B). Remove the filler, *then* close the bleed valve (valve C) and cap the bottle. If you close the bleed valve too soon, there will be pressure in the bottle and there will be a spray of foam when you remove the filler.

If you only rarely need to fill bottles, you can attach a short length (1 foot) of ¼-inch I.D. (inside diameter) poly hose to the spout of a keg's picnic tapper. This method does not purge air from the bottle, but it costs less than a quarter and will produce acceptable results for most homebrewers.

Priming Vessels/Bottling Buckets

When you're ready to bottle, you'll probably want to rack your beer to another vessel to remove settled material (thereby clarifying your beer) and to add the priming sugar. Usually a large plastic bucket is used for a priming vessel, sometimes with a valve installed for bottling.

Some homebrewers have drilled holes in their bottling buckets and attached spigots so that filling bottles is simply a matter of turning a valve on and off. This is indeed easier than using a hose with a bottling wand, but there is a risk of oxidizing the beer. The beer splashes into the bottle vigorously, which introduces excessive amounts of oxygen. Splashing and oxidation can be minimized, however, if a length of stiff tubing (brass or hard plastic) is added to the outlet of the valve. The tubing diameter should allow it to fit snugly over or inside (your choice) the outlet of the valve, and it should be a bit longer than your tallest bottle.

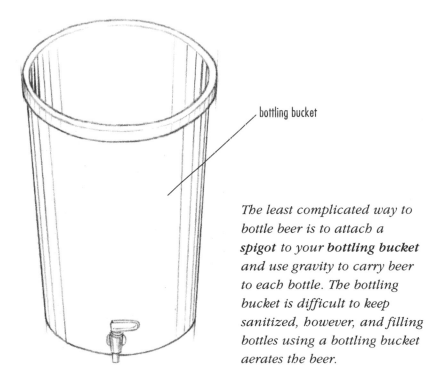

bottling bucket

*The least complicated way to bottle beer is to attach a **spigot** to your **bottling bucket** and use gravity to carry beer to each bottle. The bottling bucket is difficult to keep sanitized, however, and filling bottles using a bottling bucket aerates the beer.*

In the past, Karl has done this with great success, except for those times when the extension tube has fallen off. (Gluing the tube in place is not recommended because you will need to disassemble the valve for cleaning.) Now, he simply attaches a hose to the valve outlet, which has a much tighter fit than his filling tube, and uses a spring-loaded bottle filler on the other end. No siphon needed. Open valve. Fill bottles. (Of course, Karl now kegs everything, so this method too is obsolete.)

CAPPERS

Two types of bottle cappers are commonly used by homebrewers — a two-levered design, often referred to as the "wing" design or the "butterfly" design, and a single-levered bench capper. The two-levered models sell for as little as $10, whereas the bench cappers are typically $25 to $35.

Bench Capper

Wing Capper

Bottle cappers come in two types — bench and wing. Both are fine.

The bench cappers are usually adjustable, either by raising and lowering the platform on which the bottle sits or by raising and lowering the capping and lever housing.

Occasionally you will hear of a capper that is simply a piece of metal that fits over the cap and that you whack with a hammer, but we know of no homebrewer today who would use such a piece of trash. These break as many bottles as they seal.

CASES

Most homebrewers use cardboard boxes to hold their beer bottles, but cardboard cases tend to wear out over time and collapse. So, some of the more gung-ho home workshop owners find themselves wanting something a little sturdier. Their choice: building cases out of wood. In this way they get tough, long-lasting cases that will safely hold and transport bottles of beer for years. You too can build wooden cases, along with lids to completely protect the bottles from light exposure and to enable you to stack the cases.

Materials for a Wooden Beer Case

One 4'x8' sheet of ⅜" plywood
One 4'x4' x ⅛" sheet of paneling, masonite, waferboard, or similar material
Fourteen 90° braces
Fifty-two #6 x ⅜" wood screws
Glue and clamps

Directions

1. Cut two side pieces and the bottom pieces, 18¾" x 12" from the ⅜" plywood.
2. Cut the two end pieces, 12" x 12" from the ⅜" plywood.

3. Locate the center of the end pieces. Measure down 1¾"
   and mark the point. Mark two points 1" on either side of
   this center point. Drill at these two points with a 1¼"-
   diameter hole saw. (This will create hand holes.)
4. Trim out the rest of the hand hole with a sabre saw.
5. Glue, clamp, and square up the side pieces to the end
   pieces. (The end pieces fit between the side pieces.)
   Attach two 90° braces per corner, 3" from the edges, with
   the wood screws to provide additional strength.
6. Glue and clamp (or use very small finish nails) the
   bottom onto the side and end pieces.
7. Add two braces per side and one per end on the bottom.

Optional: You may want to glue a 2"x2" block of ⅜" plywood
per corner (and one in the center) if you're going to be setting
this on nice flooring. If it's going to sit on a concrete floor,
don't worry about it.

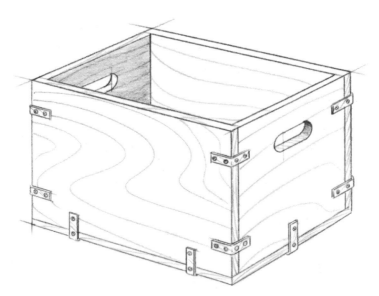

*If cardboard boxes are not good enough for you, try building
this rugged **beer case** out of plywood. It also has steel braces
for security.*

Dividers for Beer Case

1. Cut three long dividers 18"x6".
2. Cut five short dividers 12"x6".
3. Draw a 3⅛"-long line from one edge every 3" on all pieces.
4. Cut a ⅛" slot along these lines (a router works best, but a sabre saw does fine too).
5. Turn the three long dividers so the slots face up, and push a short divider down across the slots. Glue them if you wish, but it's not necessary.
6. Slide the divider assembly into the box. You may have to rasp the ends of the dividers to get it to fit.

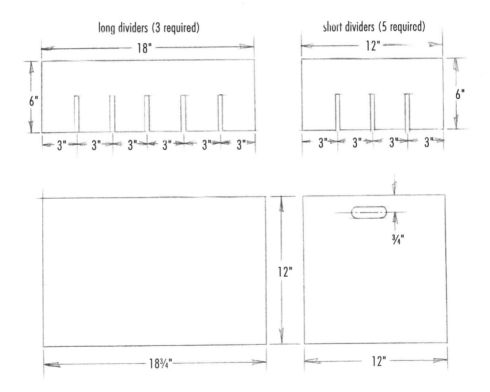

Beer case layout: The sides, bottom, and end pieces are ⅜-in. plywood. The interior dividers are made of masonite.

ALTERNATIVES TO BOTTLES

Because bottling is so much work, homebrewers are always on the lookout for ways to cut down on the labor. In this section we'll look at some approaches that are midway between the work of bottling and the cost of kegging.

Party Pig

The Party Pig made by Quoin (see Sources) is a 2½-gallon plastic tank that uses a pressure package made of citric acid and bicarbonate of soda to provide tapping pressure. Once you prime the pig, the pouch continues to expand as the volume of beer decreases until your beer is gone. The initial cost of the pig is about $35. You'll need two to handle a 5-gallon batch. You'll also need a supply of pressure pouches. Some brewpubs are starting to sell beer in the pigs, so you may be able to get a supply of pigs for less cost than you'd expect. The Party Pig is a neat idea that works well, but the cost can add up quickly if you brew a lot.

*The **Party Pig** allows you to brew 2½ gallons using a pressure pouch to provide tapping pressure.*

5-Liter Mini-Kegs

Some European breweries sell beer in 5-liter mini-kegs (also known as "party kegs" or inaccurately as "gallon cans." These cans can be used by homebrewers as an alternative to bottling. It will take about four cans to handle a typical 5-gallon batch, and you will need to get a supply of re-usable rubber bungs and a tapper. Several types of tappers are available. Plastic tappers that pump air into the can to force the beer out are inexpensive and never need additional maintenance, but they cannot keep the keg pressurized over time, and the beer will go flat overnight. Other tapper models use small CO_2 cylinders — like those used in BB guns — to provide carbonation and pressure. The better models can hold pressure for longer periods of time — several weeks or even a month or more. The secret to these is to not leave the valve open for long. Let a little CO_2 in, close the valve, and do not reopen until the beer stops pouring at an acceptable rate.

*Five-liter **mini-kegs** or "party kegs" provide an inexpensive alternative to bottling. The plastic models cannot hold pressure very long. Better ones can hold pressure for a month or more.*

The kegs can be bought for about $5 each at homebrew supply shops, or you can buy them full of beer from many retailers. Because these use CO_2 cylinders, the long-term cost is likely to be higher than for a real kegging system, although the initial cost is quite low.

Beer Balls

Coors has been selling beer in 2½-gallon or 5-gallon party balls for several years. These are round plastic containers with a tap on top. They can be used for kegging homebrew if you get a latching and tapping mechanism from The Brewery of Potsdam, N.Y. Brewers can simply pick up a ball of Coors beer and then reuse the container by fitting it with a snap cap, which sells for about $4.

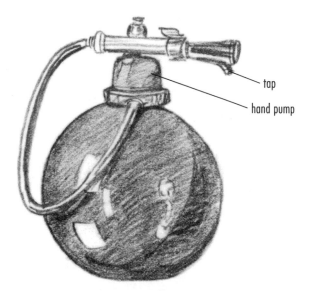

tap

hand pump

*This strange-looking device is **a party ball**. They come in 2½-gallon and 5-gallon sizes, which can be used by homebrewers for kegging their beer.*

Growlers

Several small breweries sell their beer in half-gallon jugs or bottles called "growlers." These are a perfect size for bringing your beer to a tasting or a club meeting, and they are often used by homebrewers who keg. The best ones are made of heavy glass and have a swing top with a rubber gasket, such as a Grolsch bottle.

Of all the alternatives to bottling that we have discussed, we like the Party Pig the best. We don't care for small CO_2 cylinders, and the small pressure pouches used by Quoin work very well. The pigs fit well in a refrigerator, and the cost to start pigging your beer is fairly low. Nevertheless, if it's a choice between any of these approaches and using soda kegs, we'd go with the kegs. If you do keg, the growlers are great, but we don't recommend them for all brewers because of their fairly high cost.

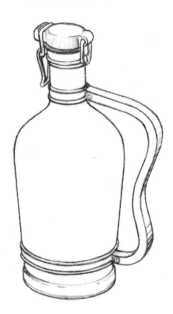

Growlers, ½-gallon jugs used by some small breweries, are a perfect size for carrying your special brew to a party.

– 10 –

KEGGING

IF THERE'S ONE GADGET that marks a transition from the casual homebrewer to the die-hard hobbyist, it's the keg. Bottles are fine when you're starting out and not sure how dedicated you are to the hobby; but once you're hooked, the advantages of kegs over bottles are just too obvious to be ignored.

When you bottle you've got 50-some bottles to wash and sanitize for every batch, and it takes a lot of time to fill and cap each one. Whereas beginning homebrewers worry about the cost of kegging setups, experienced homebrewers willingly spend the money. It's a trade-off between time and money.

There are, of course, benefits to bottles too. They're easy to carry and hand out to friends. They're easy to store for long periods of time. They're easy to send to competitions. As we've said, it's a trade-off. So let's assume you've got the homebrew bug. What does it take to put together a kegging setup?

PUTTING TOGETHER THE KEG SYSTEM

Several companies will sell you a complete, ready-to-fill kegging system for anywhere from $120 to $250. The price varies with the size of each component and whether it is new or used (you could scrounge together a system for even less).

If you're assembling the system yourself by scrounging parts or shopping around for the best prices on components, here are the things you need:

✔ Stainless-steel keg
✔ CO_2 tank
✔ Regulator with pressure gauge
✔ Connectors
✔ Tap
✔ Hoses

The kegs used by homebrewers are usually used soda kegs. These are available at many homebrew supply shops. Many homebrewers get their kegs by buying excess kegs from local soda-bottling companies, from restaurants, or from junk dealers. When you buy from these sources, you'll need to refurbish the keg. We'll get to that shortly. Homebrewers often refer to

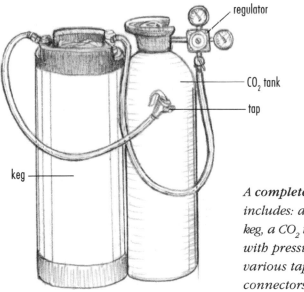

*A **complete kegging setup** includes: a stainless-steel keg, a CO_2 tank, a regulator with pressure gauge, and various taps, hoses, and connectors.*

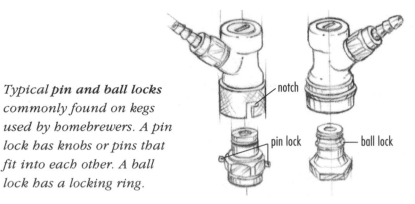

*Typical **pin and ball locks** commonly found on kegs used by homebrewers. A pin lock has knobs or pins that fit into each other. A ball lock has a locking ring.*

notch

pin lock — ball lock

these kegs as "Cornelius" kegs, after one of the companies that makes them. Yours may or may not be a Cornelius keg; it could be a Firestone or a John Wood. If you've ever thought about getting into kegging, now may be your last chance. Soda companies are increasingly abandoning kegs for plastic bags. Kegs are now easy to come by cheaply, but once the last of the soda companies switches, the supply will dry up.

There are two important things to know about any keg you're buying: size and lock type. Most homebrewers use 5-gallon kegs, the most commonly available size. You can also find 3-gallon and 10-gallon kegs. Foxx Equipment sells new kegs in either 3-gallon or 5-gallon sizes. The locks can be either the pin type or the ball type. You can tell which is which by looking at the hose connectors (fittings) on your keg. If there are two knobs (pins) sticking out from the base of one fitting and three knobs sticking out from the base of the other, it's a pin lock. You slide steel hose connectors over these pins and then twist to lock the hoses onto the keg. Ball-lock valves, which are smooth all the way around, use a locking ring to attach the hoses. Whichever type of lock you prefer, get several kegs, and make sure they all have the same type of lock (or get two CO_2 supply lines).

The CO_2 tanks are large steel cylinders containing pressurized carbon dioxide. They are available in different sizes — the smallest used by homebrewers is referred to as a 5-pound tank, the largest, a 20-pound tank. A 10-pound tank is also available.

The 20-pound tank is preferred by many of the more serious homebrewers because it means fewer trips to a gas supplier to get it filled. At the top of the CO_2 tank is a valve handle for turning the flow on and off. The regulator and gauges attach to a threaded nut on the side of the tank.

The regulator reduces the high pressure of gas coming out of the cylinder to the pressure you want going into your keg. This is accomplished simply by turning a screw on the regulator. Attached to the regulator is a gauge that shows the pressure of gas leaving the regulator. If you've got a second gauge, it shows the pressure of gas coming into the regulator (the pressure of the CO_2 tank). Many regulators also come with a check valve, or there is one attached to the gas-out line.

You'll also need a keg connector on each valve: one for the gas line to the CO_2 tank, the other to your tap. The two connectors are different, and you'll need one of each. Further, the connectors are not interchangeable, making it impossible (well, in theory it's supposed to be impossible) to connect a line to the wrong valve (assuming you put the right connector on the right line). You may also need a barbed connector to attach to your regulator.

Most homebrewers use a plastic tap faucet attached to a length of plastic hose as their tap. The plastic taps, which are inexpensive and can be taken apart for easy cleaning, are often listed in supply catalogs as "picnic faucets." A wide range of connectors and hoses is available from Foxx Equipment or from Braukunst.

CLEANING SODA KEGS

Although homebrewers often praise stainless steel because it is easily sanitized, keep in mind that older beer kegs (and some kegs from Europe) are aluminum, and some of the cleaning agents used for stainless steel can damage aluminum.

The best sanitizing solutions to use with kegs are iodophor or trisodium phosphate (TSP). Use a plastic scrubber to loosen deposits or settled matter on the insides of kegs. TSP can be left to soak in the keg; if you get a used keg, soaking it overnight or for a couple days will not hurt the surface. You can also store your unused kegs with a TSP solution in them.

Sometimes a layer of beer matter can settle and harden onto the bottom of a keg; this is referred to as "beer stone." If a beer stone begins to build up in your keg, you can remove it with an acid solution. Let the keg soak for 2 to 6 hours. Use food-grade phosphoric acid in a solution at a strength of 1.7 to 2.0 pH and a temperature of 120° to 130°F. Then scrub the stone with a plastic abrasive. The acid dairy rinse is perfect for removing a beer stone. Beverage line cleaner may also be useful.

When you're cleaning kegs, keep in mind that household bleach should never be used. Bleach is an effective sanitizer for glass and plastic surfaces, but it will corrode stainless steel. Stick to iodophor and TSP.

Note: Tanks are required to have certificates showing that they have been pressure-tested. This is done (if needed) when you fill the tank. If a tank fails a pressure test, the certifier will drill a hole in it, preventing it from being used again. It will cost about $9 to fill a 5-pound CO_2 tank.

Tanks

Very small portable CO_2 tanks, which you can fill from your larger supply tank, are also available to homebrewers who want to take a keg to a party without bringing along a big pressure tank. You can now find portable tanks in sizes as small as 3½ ounces. West Creek Home Brewing also has some nifty gadgets for handling CO_2, such as a cap for charging a PET (polyethylene terephalate) bottle to 30 psi as a portable CO_2 source.

Another source of tanks and gas is your local compressed-gas dealer. This could be a welding shop or a business dealing exclusively with compressed gas. Check your phone book for more information. These places sometimes offer what is called a "lifetime lease" on a tank. Effectively you buy a tank and every time you need a refill, you bring in the tank, pay the refill charge (for a 20-pound tank it's usually less than $10), leave the empty tank, and walk out with another filled and certified tank. You never have to worry about a bad tank — a rare event in any case. The vendor takes the empties and recertifies them (if necessary), then fills and "sells" them to someone else. A lifetime lease may cost about $75.

Refurbishing Used Kegs

Okay, you've managed to obtain some old kegs from a soda bottler . . . what next? Now, you've got to clean those kegs and replace the rubber seals.

Materials for Refurbishing a Used Keg

Rubber gasket for the lid
Rubber O-rings for the two valve fittings
Rubber O-ring for the gas dip tube
Rubber O-ring for the liquid dip tube

Most homebrew supply stores either have these parts or can get them. Foxx Equipment also sells all the gaskets as well as replacement poppets (spring-valves inside a fitting) and other parts. Gaskets cost anywhere from about 25 cents to about a dollar each, and $5 will get you a complete set. Poppets are cheap too, usually less than $2 each.

Directions

1. Release any pressure left in the keg. Use the pressure relief valve if the keg's got one; otherwise press down

with a screwdriver on the gas-in line (usually labeled, or it's the valve with 2 pins if you've got a pin-lock keg).

2. Remove the lid (also called the "closure") by lifting up on the bail (the release handle).

3. Use a wrench to remove the two valve fittings. There will be tubes attached to the fittings inside the keg. Pull these out, too.

4. Examine the poppets. If they are damaged or worn, replace them.

5. Clean the keg with TSP, B-Brite, iodophor, or similar cleaner, as described in the previous section.

6. Examine the liquid tube (the long tube) and the gas tube (the short tube). If these are plastic, consider replacing them.

7. Replace O-ring gaskets on the liquid tube and the gas dip tube.

8. Replace O-rings on the outside of the valve fittings.

9. Reassemble the tubes and fittings, screwing them back onto the keg.

10. Replace the gasket on the lid.

KEGGING ACCESSORIES

Once you've got a kegging setup, there are some neat gadgets that can help you enjoy it more, or give you some added flexibility.

Carbonator

A new little device that makes life a bit easier for folks with keg setups is the Carbonator, which allows you to take beer from the keg and store it in 2-liter plastic bottles. The Carbonator usually sells for about $11 to $12. Essentially, it is a gas ball valve fitted on a 2-liter bottle cap. To use it, fill a 2-liter bottle (precleaned, of course) with beer from the tap, then screw the Carbonator cap on instead of the regular bottle cap. Take the

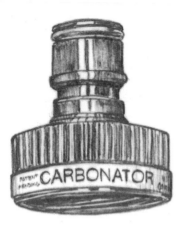

*The **Carbonator** is a nifty device that lets you store beer in 2-liter plastic bottles. Basically it's a screw-on cap with a ball valve that lets you apply CO_2 to each bottle.*

gas line from your keg and attach it to the Carbonator cap, giving the beer a fresh charge of CO_2. It works fairly well and is a lot easier to take to a picnic than lugging around the CO_2 tank, keg, bucket of ice, and so on.

Quarter-Barrels

Another often overlooked keg is the quarter-barrel. These little gems hold 7¾ gallons of beer and are excellent for the 10-gallon batch maker. You can fill the keg and have enough extra beer for one case of bottles for competitions, picnics, gifts to the authors of this book, and so on. Contact your local distributors for help in locating a legal keg. If you weren't paying attention earlier, paying the deposit on a full keg of beer, consuming the contents, and then keeping the keg is not a legal means of acquiring it. Check out scrap dealers and companies that refurbish old kegs. The keg that we acquired was fitted with a Hoff-Stevens tap (dual-pin type) with a bung (round plug) in the side. Other kegs may not have a bung but a center ball valve instead. These center-type valves also serve as the bung. Be sure to locate the right kind of tap for your keg before getting too far into the project.

To prepare the quarter-barrel for use in the homebrewing environment, first take it outside! Then attach the tap to the keg, remembering to point it away from yourself and anyone else, to vent all the pressure (and a bit of beer). A ball-type valve is easier to deal with: Lay a cloth over the valve and use a screwdriver to push down on the ball.

Keg with Bung

The next step is to get that bung out of the side of the keg. (Ball-type valve keg owners can go on to the next section.) The easiest way to get bungs out is to drill a 1" hole through the center of the bung. You can then grab it with a pair of channel lock pliers and pull it out or pry it out. The plastic burrs will rinse out easily.

Ball-Valve Kegs

Owners of this type of keg will need one or two flat-blade screwdrivers and a pair of needle-nose pliers. First you have to remove a coil of metal that seals the ball valve. Using the screwdriver(s), pry, turn, and twist the end of the coil out enough to grab it with the pliers. Pull the coil toward the center of the valve and up. It should all come out with just a bit of effort. If you have several kegs to work on, a clip remover can be made from a putty knife. Grind a hook onto one edge so that it can slip in and pull out the end of the retainer coil. Next, set a screwdriver onto one of the tabs inside the valve assembly. Tap the screwdriver with a hammer until the pins line up with the slots. The valve and dip-tube assembly should now be free to lift out.

Next, clean and sanitize everything as described in the section on Cornelius kegs (page 185 to 186). Add your freshly fermented beer to the keg and insert the bung (see Replacement Bung on page 191 to 192). If you have the valve dip-tube assembly, sanitize it and insert it until fully seated. Then, using a screwdriver and hammer, tap it clockwise until it turns no more. Artificially carbonate the beer by putting the keg in the refrigerator, attaching the keg tap, and turning on the CO_2. Pressurize to 10 to 12 psi. Leave the gas on, and the beer will carbonate in three to four days with no effort. It also will settle out during this time. Discard the first glass (or start a batch of beer with it) and enjoy!

Replacement Bung

Rather than using a new bung every time the keg is filled and having to fight to get the bung out, Karl developed a reusable, expandable bung from a synthetic rubber stopper. Synthetic rubber stoppers are used because they impart no odor.

Materials for Making a Reusable, Expandable Bung

One synthetic rubber stopper with a ¼"-diameter hole cut into it
   (see description of hole driller on page 127 to 128)
One ¼"x2"-long stainless-steel bolt and nut
Two 1¾"-diameter stainless-steel washers

Note: Use a stopper with a diameter a bit larger than that of the bung hole. Adjust the size of the stainless-steel washers if necessary.

Directions

1. Make a hole driller as described on page 127 to 128. Use a ¼" brass tube.
2. Cut a hole all the way through the center of the stopper.
3. Go to your local machine shop or welding supplier to have the bolt welded to one of the washers. (If you can weld stainless steel, then by all means do it yourself!)
4. The stainless washer and welded bolt assembly goes on the narrow end of the stopper, with the bolt running through the hole in the stopper.

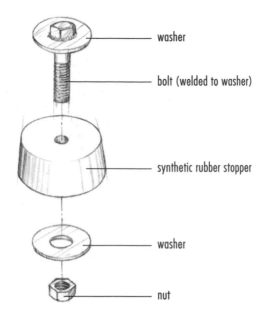

washer

bolt (welded to washer)

synthetic rubber stopper

washer

nut

*Make this **expandable and reusable bung,** and never again will you have to wrestle the keg to remove a bung.*

5. Place the other washer over the bolt and loosely thread on the nut.

6. Sanitize the entire arrangement the first time you use it by boiling for 15 minutes. This will remove any scent left in the stopper. After this, iodophor will work fine as a sanitizer.

7. Place the "bung" into the bung hole and press down as hard as possible. Turn the nut with a wrench to squeeze the stopper, making an even tighter fit; but do not overtighten.

To test the keg, we run it up to 30 psi; the pop-off valve on our setup was set to release at this pressure. The bung held fast without any leaks. To remove the stopper-bung, vent the keg and loosen the nut, then push on one side of the stopper. It should pop right out. Do not pry out the stopper with a screwdriver. You will damage the stopper (and maybe even the keg).

Jockey Boxes

The jockey box is a quick-cooling device that lets you serve cold beer from warm kegs. Basically it's an ice chest with a length of copper (or, preferably, stainless-steel) coil inside. There's a fitting for a beer hose on one side of the cooler and a tap handle on the other. When you're ready to serve beer, simply connect the beer line from your keg to the jockey box and fill the chest with ice. As the beer flows from the keg through the iced coil, it's chilled just the right amount for drinking. Jockey boxes are easy to build, but you can buy them prebuilt from North Harbor Manufacturing ($120), or from Foxx Equipment ($135 to $225).

The idea of making a jockey box from an ice chest was described by Teri Fahrendorf in *Zymurgy's* Special Issue 1992. In Teri's article, she recommended setting up the box with three tap handles (and three chilling coils) to handle multiple kegs. We think for most homebrewer applications one tap handle (maybe two) is sufficient, but if you plan to use the box for parties, then three may not be enough. Teri also recommends stainless-steel tubing for the coils. This is a good idea; if you can get stainless, use it. However, copper is very easy to find, and if the lines are cleaned quickly after use and the beer is not left to sit long in the lines, copper should not be a problem. Cleaning the lines is critical. Mix TSP with water in a keg, run some of this solution through the line under CO_2 pressure, then run water through the line to rinse.

Materials for a Jockey Box

An ice chest (48 quarts will work well for one- or two-handle boxes. It doesn't have to hold heat, so an inexpensive picnic cooler should work fine.)

Standard beer faucet and tap handle (about $15 for the faucet, and $1 for the handle)

Beer shank (the metal tube that goes through the wall, or in this case, the side of the cooler) with wall flange and jam nut (a 3" shank should be about right — these cost about $11 from Foxx)

Preformed stainless-steel or copper coil, or about 25' of ¼"-diameter copper tube

Two ¼" compression to ¼" hose barb adapters

Two ¼" compression nuts with ferrules

¼" tail piece and hex nut

Three ¼" I.D. (inside diameter) hose clamps

¼"-diameter vinyl hose, FDA (or brewery) approved (4" or so needed inside the box, plus whatever length needed from the box to the keg)

Silicone caulk

Directions

1. Drill a hole through one side of the cooler to accommodate the beer shank.
2. Drill another hole through the opposite wall to accommodate the stainless-steel or copper tubing. This is the "beer-in" side.
3. If the cooler does not have a drain valve, drill a hole at or near the bottom of the cooler to drain liquid (you may want to attach a length of hose and run it to a bucket; if so, seal it with silicone caulk).
4. Attach the beer shank to the cooler. Apply a small amount of caulk to the area around the shank, inside and out.
5. Place the jam nut on the shank on the inside of the cooler and lightly tighten.
6. Attach tail piece with the hex nut.
7. Set the coil (see page 107 to 108 on making a copper coil, if necessary) inside the box, run the tubing through the "beer-in" side hole, and caulk around the tubing, inside and out.

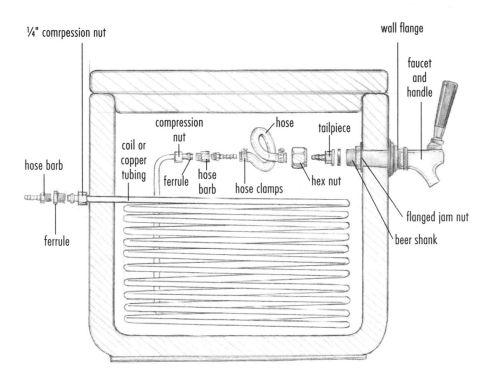

*With a **picnic-cooler jockey box** like this, you'll never have to worry about serving warm beer again.*

8. Place a ¼" compression nut and ferrule onto both ends of the copper tubing.

9. Attach a hose barb to each compression nut and tighten.

10. Attach the coil to the beer-shank tail piece with a 4" or so piece of vinyl hose and secure with hose clamps.

When you're ready to use the jockey box, run some warm TSP solution through the lines and rinse with warm water. Then simply fill the ice chest with ice, attach the beer hose from the keg to the barbed fitting on the outside of the box, and you're ready to go. We also recommend after using the jockey box that you run warm TSP solution through the lines and rinse prior to storing.

Using Wooden Casks

There's a great deal of romance associated with aging and serving beer from wooden barrels. Yet for all the mystique, homebrewers seem more concerned about the possible risks of infection from hard-to-sanitize surfaces, uncontrollable flavor characteristics, oxidation, and, generally, difficult storage and handling techniques.

Because wooden barrels are used more often for aging than for dispensing the beer, they may fit better in another chapter, but we've chosen to talk about them here because many homebrewers seem to think of them much like kegs, and there is some interest in using them to tap beer "from the wood."

Information about using barrels is scarce in the homebrewing literature, and most of it is quite negative, so Jim Mosser of the Brewlab in Allentown, Pennsylvania, decided to get some oak barrels and try them out himself. He used 3-gallon American oak barrels with a charred surface. The barrels were first filled with water and allowed to sit for several hours to let the wood swell and stop any leaks. Jim then filled the barrels with hot water and a cleaner called "Barokleen," a blend of soda ash and lye. He left this in the barrel for three days and then repeated the process to leach tannins out of the wood. Jim then rinsed the barrels thoroughly with cold water several times over several days, always leaving the barrels full. He then sanitized the barrels with a blend of sodium metabisulphite and citric acid and rc-rinsed the barrels several times with cold water. He then brewed a batch of beer, filled the barrels, and attached airlocks. The beer was left in the barrels for 10 days and then bottled.

Jim says that the first batch had a noticeable oak character that mellowed after aging in the bottle. Subsequent batches have less oak character.

One thing to keep in mind with barrels is to always leave them full, either with beer or water. A barrel that is allowed to dry out will develop leaks. American oak barrels are available from several sources, including Lehman's Hardware and

Cumberland General Store. Both sources also sell faucets, if you're interested in experimenting with dispensing from the wood. Jim does not recommend this, because of carbonation problems, so you're on your own.

Serving beer from the wood is done in England and is described in Terry Foster's book, *Pale Ale*. In England they vent negative pressure through the bung to keep the beer flowing.

Modifying Refrigerators for Kegs

In Chapter 8 we talked about using refrigerators as rooms where you can keep a fermenter at a constant temperature. In this chapter the focus is a bit different, if more familiar. We're going to talk about using your refrigerator to store beer in kegs. The temperature of a normal operating refrigerator is likely to be about the temperature at which you want to serve beer. But if you're using the same refrigerator for both fermenting and serving, by all means adapt the temperature control as we discussed earlier.

The first order of business for accommodating kegs is to remove the shelves from the refrigerator. A soda keg sits about 2½ feet high, a 5-pound CO_2 tank about 1½ feet high. You'll probably want these to sit upright, so removing the shelves is a necessity. You also may want to look at the bottom shelf to see how it's supported. Often the bottom shelves are made of glass and are supported on the sides by molded plastic and sometimes in the middle by a brace. You may want to remove this shelf and replace it with something a bit sturdier, such as a piece of ½-inch plywood braced under the middle and sides by 2-inch by 4-inch braces. A keg weighs about 50 pounds when full, so the shelf and supports need to be pretty strong.

If you find yourself running out of space, you can either buy a second refrigerator or extend the one you have. In *Dave Miller's Homebrewing Guide,* Miller explains how to extend your refrigerator by removing the door, building a small insulated addition, and attaching the door to that. A second refrigerator, however, has the benefit of allowing you to set two temperature ranges.

Most homebrewers like adding tap handles to the outside of the fridge so they don't have to open the door every time they want a beer. This is a fairly straightforward modification. The tap handles and shanks that go through the door are available from Foxx Equipment. The size you get will depend on the thickness of your refrigerator door (or side wall). If you're drilling through the side wall, be aware that some refrigerators have gas lines running in the walls. If you puncture one of these, the refrigerator will be useless. If the side of the refrigerator is warm to the touch, it probably contains gas lines.

Materials for Modifying a Refrigerator

Beer shank
Wall flange
Flanged jam nut
Tail piece and hex nut
Beer faucet
Tap handle
Drip tray

Directions

1. Measure the thickness of the refrigerator wall before ordering your shank. You'll probably want about a 4" or 5" shank, but the length depends on the thickness of the refrigerator wall.
2. Drill a hole through the refrigerator wall to accommodate the shank.
3. Put the wall flange onto the shank.
4. Insert the shank through the door.
5. Apply a small amount of caulk around the area where

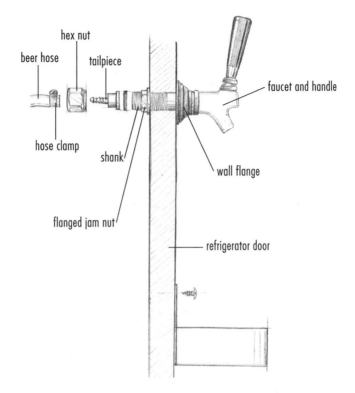

hex nut

beer hose   tailpiece

faucet and handle

hose clamp

shank

wall flange

flanged jam nut

refrigerator door

*If you store your beer in a keg in a refrigerator, **install a tap** on the door or side wall. You won't have to open the door each time you want a beer.*

 the shank passes through the door, inside and out, and
 secure with the flanged jam nut on the inside.

6. Attach the tail fitting with the hex nut onto the shank on
 the inside.

7. Screw the faucet onto the outside of the refrigerator.

8. Screw the knob onto the faucet.

9. Screw the drip tray onto the refrigerator about 1 foot or
 so below the faucet (allow enough space to accommodate your largest beer glass).

10. Attach your beer line to the barbed tail fitting, then
 tighten the hose clamp.

11. Connect to your keg and enjoy.

Transferring Liquid under Pressure

Once you have a kegging system with a CO_2 tank and regulator, you can use pressurized carbon dioxide to move liquids from one vessel to another without having to rely on siphons and gravity. For example, you can force-rack beer from one carboy to another under CO_2 pressure, avoiding the worries of starting the siphon and reducing oxidation risk by purging vessels with a blanket of CO_2 gas. Transfers can thus take place in a "closed" environment, which means that the vessels are never open to airborne contamination risks. The idea is simple: Seal up the container holding the liquid; attach a tube from the liquid to the empty vessel; attach a gas-in line to the carboy cap, keg, or whatever; and slowly open the gas line. If you're doing this with a carboy cap, you may need to hold the cap down. Several other applications for pressure transfers are described by Bennet Dawson in the July/August 1994 issue of *Brewing Techniques,* including a way of harvesting yeast from a carboy.

– 11 –

GROWING AND
DRYING HOPS

Hop vines grow in most of North America (roughly the area between the 30th and 50th latitudes). We do not present a comprehensive discussion of hops and their cultivation here; rather, we focus on several gadgets that help those homebrewers who do grow their own hops. A more detailed discussion of hops is available in Mark Garetz's book *Using Hops*. The best source for hop rhizomes (stem tubers) in the United States is Freshops (see Suppliers).

TRELLISES AND POLES

Hop vines grow to a length of 25 feet and twine around poles or strings. In the first year of growth for a new plant, a 6-foot-long pole or string will suffice; but in subsequent years, when the plant is established, longer lengths will be needed.

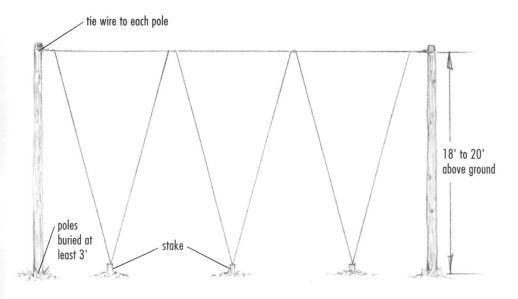

*A **hop trellis** is simple to build and will provide great support for your own hop plants. Plant one hop plant per stake.*

A hop trellis is a good idea. To make one, stick two long poles (15 to 20 feet in length) in the ground about 20 feet apart. Attach a guy wire between the two tops and run strings at angles down to stakes positioned midway between the poles. Of course, one of the problems with such a trellis is that when hop harvesting takes place at the end of the season, reaching the upper parts of the vine can be a problem. You can pull the entire trellis down, cut the guy wire, use a very tall ladder or stilts, or rent a cherry picker.

One way around the problem is to build a structure that fits around the hop pole and can easily be lowered to the ground at the end of the season. This can be done by attaching a pulley to the top of the pole. Then, with a length of rope passing through the pulley and attached to the top framework, the structure can be raised and lowered at will. Because the pole may be as much as 20 feet high, however, you will also need guy wires to keep it from shifting in the wind.

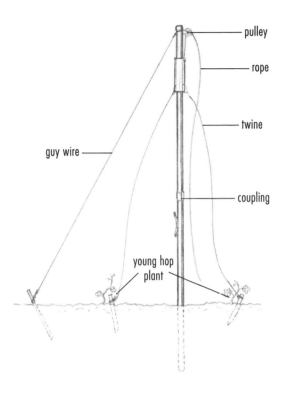

pulley

rope

twine

guy wire

coupling

young hop plant

*Because hop plants grow 25 ft. high, a **hop pole with a pulley** is a good idea. This structure can be raised and lowered to make harvesting easier.*

Materials for a Hop Pole

Two 12' lengths of 2"-diameter galvanized pipe, threaded
One coupling
One short length of 3"-diameter or larger PVC pipe
Three 30' lengths of cable
One 45' length of rope
Three 18"-long tent stakes (or lengths of rebar)
Twelve to fifteen tent stakes
Twelve to fifteen 30' lengths of twine or rope
One pulley

Directions

1. Dig a hole in the ground about 4' deep, around which you will plant the hops. The pole will be the two lengths of pipe. Connect the two lengths together with the coupling.

Drill three ¼" holes, spaced 60 degrees apart, at the top of the pole.

2. Attach the guy wires to these holes. Drill another hole near the top and bolt the pulley into it. Drill about 15 to 20 ³⁄₁₆" holes around the PVC pipe. Slip the PVC pipe over the bottom of the pole.

3. Attach one length of the rope to the PVC pipe and thread the rope through the pulley. Plant the pole in the ground and pack dirt (or concrete) around it. Attach the bottoms of the guy wires to long stakes (or rebar) in the ground. Tie lines of twine to the PVC. Pull the rope, raising the PVC with twine lines up to the top of the pole. Tie the rope securely, and then run each twine line to a tent stake.

HOP DRYER

Hops can easily be dried for storage with a dehydrator that is adapted from one used for preserving fruits and vegetables. It is a simple device. Several trays hold the hops, and a heater on the bottom of the unit generates warm air. This air rises by convection, passing through the trays and drawing out the water. A good dehydrator must have a variable temperature control because a temperature range between 110° and 160°F will be needed. Aromatic hops should be dried at 120° to 140°F; the lower end of the scale is preferred to prevent loss of essential oils. Bittering hops can be dried at a slightly higher temperature than aromatics, but since you've gone to all the trouble to grow your own, why lose any of your hard work?

Some commercially available dehydrators come with a base heater unit and two "food" trays for under $100; additional trays are extra. Other, more expensive units run $200 and up. They all work the same way and, set at the same level, dehydrate at about the same rate. Dehydrators are also easy to build out of white pine, a heating element, an optional fan, and, of course, some kind of control. Clear white pine is best, but small knots in the wood are acceptable. Yellow pine or knotty white pine should be avoided, as they release lots of aromatics from the resins in the wood.

Adding trays is simple. Usually about 10 trays per heating unit is the maximum, but it depends on the base unit. If your unit has fan(s) to force air through and a large enough heater, then you can add even more trays. However, you must be careful not to load the trays too full because it can stop the air flow; even a two-tray unit will not function well without air flow.

A lid for the top tray is optional, but it's a good way to keep flies and other pests out, plus you can use it to help adjust the air flow. By partially closing off the top you will have higher temperature inside, although a bit slower air flow. Conversely, by opening the top all the way you will lower the air temperature passing through the trays, but the air flow will increase. This can also be accomplished by adjusting the heater unit. It all depends on what you want to do. Of course, if it's a purchased unit, be sure to read the instructions.

The bottom of the trays should be covered with an FDA–approved mesh, and it should be heat-resistant. Obviously any mesh or slat system that will hold the items for drying and allow air to pass through will work, but certain materials should be avoided.

Aluminum or galvanized window screening should not be used, as it can react with the items being dried — especially if the items are high in moisture and are alkaline or highly acidic. We don't have adequate information on fiberglass window screening, so we will not recommend its use. Plastic mesh works well, as long as it is FDA–approved and heat-resistant. Rubbermaid manufactures a 2-foot-wide Aero-Liner mesh that is steam cleanable and sold as shelving liners to restaurant/bar supply houses. It's not too expensive. And it can easily be stapled to the inside of the wood trays.

Our heating element was made from nickel-chromium wire, also known as "ni-chrome wire." This wire comes in various sizes and has a rating of a certain number of ohms per foot. Ours was rated at 1.2 ohms per foot. This wire may be a bit tricky to locate, but calling a local refrigeration repair shop might help. Commercial ice makers use ni-chrome wire to cut sheets of ice into cubes.

Light bulbs are not recommended as heating elements because you'll have to block the light from whatever you're drying. Light can affect the quality of the hops; so rather than try to eliminate the light, we decided life would be easier if we were not producing it in the first place — thus the ni-chrome wire. Our heater control is an incandescent light dimmer, which is rated at 600 watts. We designed in a nice margin of safety and decided that a 300-watt heating element would be the maximum for our base unit. We used basic knowledge of electricity as represented in the two formulas below.

$$\text{Power (watts)} = \text{Volts} \times \text{Amps}$$
$$\text{Volts} = \text{Amps} \times \text{Resistance}$$

Plugging in the knowns and a bit of math later:

$$300 \text{ Watts} / 120 \text{ Volts} = 2.5 \text{ Amps}$$
$$120 \text{ Volts} / 2.5 \text{ Amps} = 48 \text{ Ohms worth of wire will be needed.}$$

Our wire resistance is 1.2 ohms per foot (yours may differ), so:

$$48 \text{ Ohms} / 1.2 = 40 \text{ feet of wire}$$

This wire is routed back and forth across the lower inside of the base unit and is connected to the incandescent light dimmer and a power cord. You cannot solder ni-chrome wire, so use wire nuts or crimp connectors instead. We had a problem, however: 40 feet of wire means over 40 runs back and forth inside our 12-inch by 12-inch base unit. Rather than do this, we carefully wound the wire around a ½-inch-diameter piece of pipe to make a coil, which we run back and forth only eight times. Well worth the time making the coil.

Materials for the Base Unit of a Dehydrator

Four 1"x8"x12"-long mostly clear white pine boards
Several 1"x10⅞"-long slats (white pine)
Four 1"x1"x1¾"-long legs
Several nonmetallic stand-offs (insulators) (bakelite, ceramic, etc.) — barrier strips work well too
Calculated length of ni-chrome wire (see text) — 40 feet in our case
A 600-watt incandescent light dimmer
A grounded power cord
Wire nuts
Glue and screws

Directions

1. Cut out the four boards to make the sides of the base.
2. Cut a dado ¾" wide by ⅜" deep on one end of each board.
3. Cut a mounting hole for the dimmer.
4. Assemble the four side pieces with glue and screws, the non-dado end fitting into the dado of the next piece (half-lap joints), as shown in the illustration on page 209.
5. Mount five stand-offs evenly across the inside of one side, 2" from the bottom.
6. Mount four stand-offs evenly across the inside of the opposite side, 2" from the bottom.
7. Slightly stretching out the ni-chrome coil, run between the stand-offs as shown in the illustration on page 209. Just run it evenly across the inside of the base unit.
8. Drill a hole in the bottom of the base and feed the power cord through.

9. Attach the ground to the ground lug of the dimmer unit.

10. Attach the hot lead (usually the black lead) of the power cord to one wire of the dimmer, and secure with a wire nut.

11. Connect the other lead from the dimmer to one end of the ni-chrome coil, and secure with a wire nut.

12. Connect the other lead of the power cord to the other end of the ni-chrome coil, and secure with a wire nut.

13. Glue and clamp the four legs on the inside corner with ½" of leg extending below the bottom of the unit.

14. Install the slats 1" from the top of the base unit, leaving about a ½" gap between. This is to prevent fingers and other body parts from coming in contact with the hot wire. You can omit the slats, but remember that we told you to put them in!

Materials for the Tray Assembly of a Dehydrator

Four 1"x2"x12" sides, mostly clear white pine
Four 1"x1"x1¾" legs, white pine
12"x12" mesh (FDA–approved, please)
Glue and screws

Directions

1. Cut the sides and build, following the base assembly instructions.

2. Install the legs on the inside corners, leaving ½" extending below the sides.

3. Cut corners of the mesh so it fits around the legs on the inside of the tray.

4. Install the mesh on the inside of the tray, as in the illustration on page 209.

5. Staple the mesh in place.

6. The legs may need to be rasped down so they will fit snugly inside the previous tray or base.

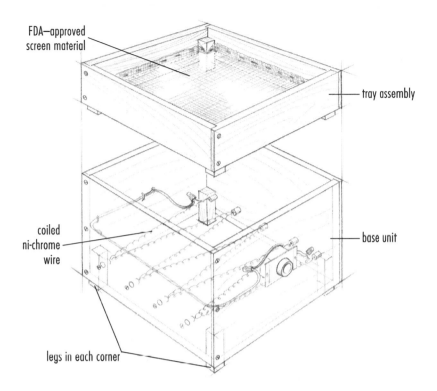

FDA–approved screen material

tray assembly

coiled ni-chrome wire

base unit

legs in each corner

*The **base unit** of a dehydrator can be made easily from clear white pine, a grounded power cord, a 600-watt light dimmer, and a length of nickel-chromium wire for a heating element. The tray assembly for your dehydrator is assembled from clear white pine and FDA–approved screen material.*

Outside finish is optional, but do not finish the inside unless you use something that is FDA–approved. The finishes used on wooden salad bowls may work fine. We decided it wasn't worth our time (and might even prove us to be wrong), so we left the wood bare. It works great for us.

Another option is to add a fan or two to the bottom of the base unit to force air through the trays. You really don't need to do this unless you are running more than 10 trays, or all your trays are heavily loaded, in which case it is better to build another dehydrator.

– 12 –

Yeast Culturing

One area that offers a homebrewer the greatest potential for improving beer quality while reducing brewing costs is yeast culturing. However, yeast culturing does require some equipment that a novice is unlikely to have. It also requires scrupulous sanitation and an understanding of sterile techniques. Before delving into equipment needed for yeast culturing, we'll begin with an examination of yeast propagation and reuse.

Why Culture?

Most brewers should ask themselves why they want to culture. It's more convenient to simply buy yeast packets from the homebrew shop and add them directly to the fermenter. Yet there are times when certain styles and variations become easier to brew authentically with cultured yeast that may be unavailable at a local supply shop. Regular users of specialty yeast strains also can realize substantial cost savings over time by using a single packet for dozens of batches. Brewers in areas that are not served by large homebrew supply stores either must go to mail-order yeast sources or learn to develop their own library of yeast cultures. In hot-weather months, mail order becomes even less attractive, and a library of cultures becomes a necessity.

Although yeast culturing initially may seem difficult or strange, anyone can learn to culture yeasts and maintain a simple bank of different strains. By culturing your yeast, you gain a better understanding of yeast and its role in brewing. You can also do what commercial breweries do: develop a single "house" strain of yeast that you use for all (or most) of your beers. Proper sanitation, and an eye toward maintaining the proper environment for healthy yeast growth, are the keys to successfully maintaining a yeast strain over a long period of time.

MAKING A STARTER

To make a simple starter, mix 2 cups of water with 5 rounded tablespoons of dry malt extract, boil in a saucepan for 15 minutes, cover, and cool. There is no need to use hops for a starter, but some homebrewers do. The liquid yeast should be allowed to rise to room temperature before pitching. Pour the cooled wort into a sanitized bottle, add the liquid yeast, and attach an airlock.

You can aerate the wort before pitching by shaking the bottle. In three to four days (maybe less), the starter should be up to full kraeusen and ready to pitch. It's time to brew!

REPITCHING YEAST

The simplest method of yeast culturing is to repitch it from a previous batch. This is done by siphoning the beer out of the fermenter and pouring a freshly made wort on top of the layer of yeast at the bottom of the fermenter. Although yeast from either the primary or secondary fermenter will work, the trub from a primary fermenter may have more material other than yeast, such as settled hops and proteins. The secondary fermenter contains far less of these other particles, and the layer will be made up mostly of yeast.

Repitching works very well provided you sanitize everything that will be coming into contact with the cool wort as it makes its way to the fermenter. Minimizing air contact with the yeast is a good idea. The two-hole carboy cap can be helpful here because there is only a small opening to allow air to pass through during the emptying and filling.

Yeast can be repitched from batch to batch several times, but eventually you reach a limit as the yeast starts to degrade (especially if you let the fermenter temperature get too high). You should be able to get three to four repitches, although some brewers do six or more consecutive batches. One drawback to repitching is that you need to have a regular brew schedule so that you are brewing one batch of beer as the previous batch is ready to rack out of the fermenter.

Saving Yeast

Some homebrewers save small samples of the yeast starter before pitching. To do this, sanitize a container, then flame the mouth of the starter vessel with a butane lighter (or other flame) and pour some of the yeast starter into the sanitized container. Seal the container, label it, and refrigerate it.

When you are ready to reuse the yeast, allow it to warm to room temperature and add it to a freshly made starter wort (as described earlier). If you save yeast from a starter that is at high kraeusen, your container is going to be building pressure, even if refrigerated (this is especially true for small containers). So, for the first week you will need to vent the pressure every day. Open the lid just enough until it hisses, then close it and return it to the refrigerator.

We like to use culture tubes (see page 214) for storing our samples. They have a screw-on cap and take up very little room in the refrigerator. In *The Homebrewer's Companion,* Charlie Papazian recommends maintaining a stock of yeast cultures by keeping the cultures in beer bottles with attached airlocks in the refrigerator.

CULTURE TUBES

Some liquid yeast vendors, such as Yeast Lab, sell cultures in 50 ml plastic, screw-top vials. These are great because you can buy the yeast, grow a starter, sanitize the vial, and save a sample of the yeast. The vial can be sanitized with either bleach or io-dophor, but not with heat.

If you are looking into culturing on a more serious level, the best containers to use are heat-resistant glass culture tubes — test tubes with threaded tops that accept a cap (see illustration on page 214). Be sure to get caps that are autoclaveable (able to resist heat). Any size tube will work, but the 15 mm by 150 mm tubes are about the smallest that we recommend, and 18 mm by 150 mm are our favorite. Some tubes have a frosted portion on which you can write a culture code or name. These are nice, but if they cost more, it's not worth the extra cost. Masking tape or peel-off labels work just as well.

When autoclaving (see page 216 to 219), do not screw the cap on tightly. Just thread it on loosely and set the tube at a slant inside the pressure cooker. A piece of metal, glass, or even another culture tube can be used to prop up the cap end of the tube. The idea is to keep the cap end up and out of the water. (A brass rack can be designed easily, bent, and soldered into an appropriate stand if desired.) When your autoclave is cool, remove the autoclave lid and tighten the caps. Wrap a piece of tape around the tube and cap to seal it. That way you will know which tubes you've sterilized and are ready for use and which tubes are not to be used (also, it prevents the caps from coming loose).

All homebrewers should keep a small supply of sterile, sealed tubes for taking yeast samples from an excellent bottle-conditioned beer. A word of caution about getting yeast from commercial beers: Some beer makers like to add a different yeast at bottling time, so what you are sampling may not be the yeast that produces the beer's signature flavors and aromas.

Culture tubes are extremely useful for making slants, which are culture tubes containing a gelatinized medium (see page 215) that have been set at an angle before the medium solidified. This gives a larger surface area for the yeast to grow on in relation to the small diameter of the culture tube.

PETRI DISHES

As you progress into yeast culturing, you'll need several petri dishes — shallow dishes that hold a gelatinized medium and a cover. These dishes are available in presterilized, disposable plastic, or autoclaveable glass (Pyrex or Kimax). The usual size is 100 mm by 15 mm.

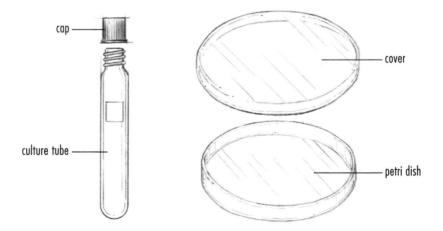

*To culture yeast you will need a supply of **glass culture tubes**, which come with a screw-on cap, or **glass petri dishes**, which come with their own cover.*

GELATINIZED MEDIUM

There are several ways to make a gelatinized medium for use with petri dishes and slants, and we are going to talk about two of them here. If the temperature where you are storing the dishes and slants during the growing phase is below 70°F, you can use two packets of unflavored gelatin added to a cup of standard starter wort. Just add it with the dry malt extract when making the starter, then sterilize (see page 216 to 219). If the temperature runs above 70°F the gelatin will liquefy, making it a poor choice. In this case one rounded tablespoon of powdered agar should be used per cup of starter wort in place of the gelatin. If you're not sure which to use, play it safe and use the agar. You can also save some money by going to an international food store and buying agar agar (not a misprint: "agar agar" is correct!). It is significantly less expensive than research-grade agar, and it comes in a lump instead of a powder; just cut off approximately a tablespoon's worth. It will dissolve when heated in the wort. Incidentally, one cup of medium is enough to do 10 petri dishes or 20 culture tubes.

Why do we need to use a gelatinized medium? For the simple reason that it is easier to identify contaminants or a good yeast colony growth when it is only on the surface of the medium rather than growing throughout it. Not convinced? Go ahead and try to isolate a single yeast colony as it floats around in a liquid medium. You'll be dumping the culture and going with a gelatinized medium before you can pronounce *Saccharomyces Cerevisiae* correctly!

MISCELLANEOUS ITEMS

If you're diving into yeast cultures, you will need an inoculation loop, a culture scalpel, and a flame source. The loop is usually a simple stainless-steel wire inserted into a wooden handle

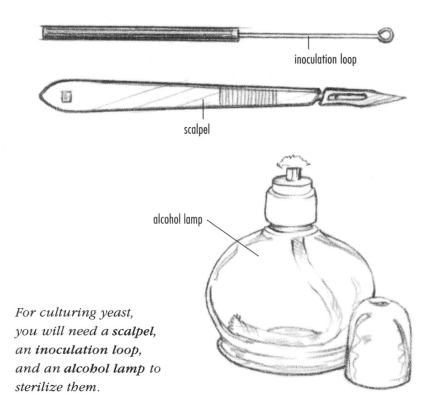

inoculation loop

scalpel

alcohol lamp

For culturing yeast, you will need a scalpel, an inoculation loop, and an alcohol lamp to sterilize them.

with the other end of the wire bent into a circle. The scalpel is a long thin wire inserted into a handle with the other end of the wire sporting a sharp blade. The flame source can be either an alcohol lamp, Bunsen burner, propane torch, or even a butane lighter. Any flame that does not leave soot (candles or matches are out) can be used. If soot gets on the medium, it is difficult to spot contaminants.

STERILIZATION

For the serious culturist, an autoclave is almost mandatory. You don't need to go out and spend lots of money, but you should invest in a good-quality pressure cooker with a gauge. One that holds four 32-ounce jars is adequate for yeast culturing needs.

These cost around $100 to $115 and are great for general canning needs as well. If you are a gardener or do lots of canning, spend the extra money and get one that holds seven 32-ounce jars. You won't regret it when you get a bumper crop of tomatoes. Sizes larger than this require special burners (such as the canning element discussed in Chapter 6) or need to sit over two burners and, therefore, are not as practical. Regardless of the kind of pressure cooker you use, be sure that it has a plate, or riser, on the bottom so that your glass items do not come in direct contact with the bottom of the pressure cooker. You will be filling that area with water, and glass vessels tend to break if heated directly.

You will also need an autoclaveable container to hold your starter. You can get a 750 ml Erlenmeyer flask, but we like the type of bottle that corn syrup comes in. It matters little; just get something that fits nicely in the pressure cooker, is heat resistant,

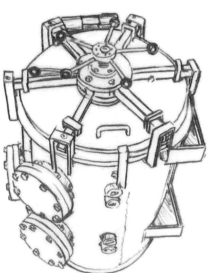

*For the serious yeast culturist, a **pressure cooker** (left) can serve as an autoclave. The **professional autoclave** (right) is a bit out of reach for most of us.*

and can take a stopper and an airlock. Glass vessels are fine, but if you wish to spend some extra dollars to know that it will survive many autoclaving runs, anything made with Pyrex or Kimax is an excellent choice.

To sterilize a starter and some tubes, first make a starter as mentioned on page 211 (you only need to boil it for a couple of minutes to make sure the dry malt extract is well dissolved). Cool the wort and pour it into your clean starter vessel, leaving the break material in the saucepan. The vessel does not need to be sanitized prior to this, just clean. Place the starter vessel and wort into the pressure cooker and then pour in water until it comes up to the bottom plate. You can fill the pressure cooker with as many starter vessels as it can hold, but save some space for a few culture tubes. Put on the lid and turn the heat to medium-high. You don't want it to heat too quickly. Let the pressure cooker vent air until it is producing a fair amount of steam; then close the vent. If you have an electric stove, start reducing the heat as it gets close to 15 psi (electric stoves take longer to adjust than gas stoves). You want to hold the pressure cooker at 15 psi for 30 minutes. When the time is up, turn off the heat and allow the pressure cooker to return to room temperature. Do not force cool the cooker, because you could break glass items. When the pressure cooker is cool enough to touch, open it and remove the items.

Sterilizing Slants and Petri Dishes

Simply fill the clean petri dishes with a thin layer (no more than half-full) of medium (agar or gelatin with wort), cover, and set carefully into the pressure cooker autoclave. Fill the culture tubes one-third of the way and set at an angle inside the pressure cooker autoclave. Add water and sterilize for 30 minutes at 15 psi. Let the cooker sit until totally cool and the medium has become firm.

Some homebrewers find it is easier to sterilize empty petri dishes and culture tubes because they can move the pressure cooker around without having to worry about spilling the medium before it sets up. If you go this route, you will need to have the wort for the dishes or slants in an easily pourable vessel, such as an Erlenmeyer flask. Fill the flask with your culture medium and sterilize it along with the dishes and tubes. In this instance, the tubes can be stored upright in the cooker to save room. Again, add water and sterilize for 30 minutes at 15 psi. Let the cooker cool to touch, then wipe it down with iodophor and take it to your clean work environment (see next section) for pouring the medium. (Don't forget to sanitize your hands.) Next, open the cooker and remove the sterilized items. With one hand, lift the lid from a petri dish just enough to pour in a layer of medium (no more than half-full). Now quickly close the dish and move on to the next dish. By the way, a slant is made by removing the cap from a culture tube, filling the tube one-third of the way with medium, recapping, and then setting it at an angle to cool.

MAINTAINING A CLEAN WORK ENVIRONMENT

Before we get into in-depth culturing, let's take a look at the work environment. It will become a critical factor now that we have lots of clean items — some sterilized, some just sanitized. How are we going to keep them clean and contaminant-free while all around us are lots of bacteria and mold and fungus spores just looking for a place to live and grow? Short of building or using an extremely expensive clean room, there is no way to get rid of all of them, but they can be greatly reduced. Here are several steps the homebrewer can take to reduce the level of airborne contamination.

Kitchen Table Method

Going with the "simpler is better" theme, let's start with the kitchen table. First, get a spray bottle that can be adjusted to a fine mist. Fill it with a 10 percent bleach-and-water solution. Label this clearly so you know what's in it. Turn off all sources of moving air, such as the furnace, air-conditioner, fans, and even the refrigerator. You want as little air movement as possible. If your kitchen has doors, close them (and lock them to keep out other family members, pets, or neighbors while you work). This is also not the time for a glass of beer. Spray the work surface with a fine mist of the bleach solution. Do not soak it. Then lightly mist the air in the room again with the bleach solution. As the mist settles, it will take the dust particles out of the air. While the mist is settling, sanitize your hands (or wear sanitized gloves). It's also a good idea to wear freshly laundered clothes. Your work area is now ready; just don't breathe on the table or any of the items because you will be one of the largest sources of contamination in the room.

Glove Box

If using the kitchen is impractical, or if you feel you cannot control the level of contaminants in the area, the next-best solution may be a glove box. The idea is simple: The interior is sealed off from the outside world while you do your work inside the box. Accordingly, the glove box needs to be large enough to deal with all the equipment you will be using *plus* allowing enough room to work. In our case, because we were transferring all the material except the pressure cooker into the box, it had to measure 3 feet by 2 feet by 16 inches high. The sides and bottom can be glass, Plexiglas, wood, or other material, but the top should be Plexiglas for obvious reasons. Seal all joints with caulk or tape. If you use wood, paint the interior wood surface with a high-gloss oil paint, which will make it

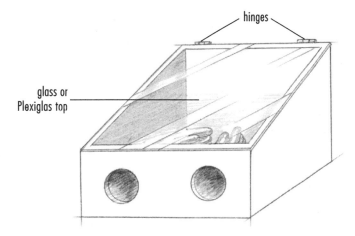

hinges

glass or
Plexiglas top

If you're worried about contaminants in your kitchen, try building a simple glove box.

easier to clean and sanitize. You will also need a way of getting your hands into the box, so cut holes in the front and tape a pair of long-armed rubber gloves to the holes. If you make the box too deep, you will not be able to use the gloves to reach items in the back of the box.

To use the glove box, first scrub your hands and arms and sanitize them. All surfaces inside the box need to be sprayed with a 10 percent bleach solution, and everything going in must be sprayed with the bleach solution as well. Metal objects, however, must be sanitized with iodophor. Once everything is in the box, mist the air in the box and close it. Let it settle for a few minutes and then begin your work.

Laminar-Flow Hood

An alternate method is to build a laminar-flow hood. These rely on High Efficiency Particulate Air (HEPA) filters to provide a sterile air flow across the work area, blowing contaminants away. HEPA filters range from 0.1 to 0.3 microns and tend to be very expensive, so a prefilter is needed to clean out much

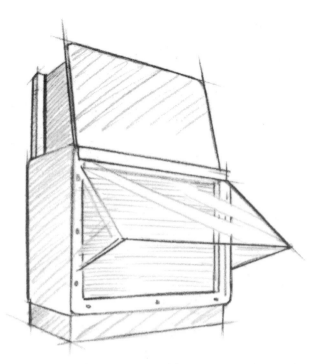

A laminar-flow hood relies on HEPA filters to provide sterile air flow across the work area.

of the dust and larger particles from the air before they reach the HEPA filter. Again, size depends on your work area. The smallest HEPA filter commonly available is a 12-inch by 12-inch, 0.3-micron filter that costs nearly $100. American Air Filter sells a 12-inch by 24-inch HEPA filter for $47.

SINGLE COLONY ISOLATION

Now that we've discussed a clean, sanitized work area, we are ready to move past the simple issues of yeast saving to enter the next and more complex step of yeast culturing. We are going to try to isolate a single yeast colony and grow it into a usable strain. Remember that all this work is done in your clean work environment.

Materials for Isolating a Single Colony of Yeast

Yeast source, either a purchased tube or a sample
from bottle-conditioned beer
Three sterile petri dishes with medium
Flame source

Directions

1. Flame the inoculating loop until it is red hot. Lift the lid off a petri dish just enough to get the loop in and cool it on the sterile medium.
2. Get a small sample of the yeast. If you have a liquid yeast sample: Dip the loop into the liquid. If you have yeast from a slant: Scrape up a few cells and recap.
3. Lift the petri dish cover enough to let the loop in. Streak the loop back and forth across the medium in a figure "S" pattern (see the illustration), and quickly cover again.
4. Repeat with two more dishes.
5. Allow the plates to sit in a warm area (60°–70°F) for two to three days.

You should see white or cream-colored streaks or dots where you streaked the yeast onto the medium. If you see any other colored areas — cottony or hairy-looking growth — you have contamination. If the contamination is at the edge of a dish but the yeast areas look good, you can transfer some of these colonies to a new sterile dish. Just don't touch the contaminated spot. If all the plates are contaminated throughout the yeast area, discard all dishes and obtain a new yeast sample.

A Starter or Micro Starter

Now that you have a dish with growing yeast colonies, you need to grow it out to a starter. To grow the yeast from petri dish to a full beer starter, we need to step it up a few times. We

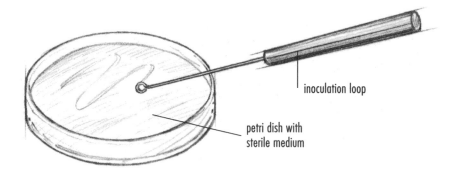

*Using an **inoculation loop** to spread a small sample of yeast on the sterile medium.*

start with a micro starter, which is nothing more than a very small amount of sterile wort in a small sterile container. Any flask size between 100 ml and 250 ml with an autoclaveable cap works very well (and you might as well get several, as they are handy for a number of things). Make 500 ml of starter wort (no agar or gelatin). Put 50 to 75 ml into the small flask, cap loosely, and put the rest of the starter wort into a larger flask (syrup bottle), which you cap loosely or cover with aluminum foil. Sterilize them both as mentioned earlier (30 minutes at 15 psi) and let cool. Seal the large vessel and refrigerate it. Later you will use the large vessel as a standard starter.

In your clean environment area, flame the inoculation loop, cool it either on the sterile medium of a petri dish or by placing it in the sterile wort in the small flask. Open the petri dish, then select and scrape up a small, healthy yeast colony. Open the flask and pass the mouth of the flask through the flame. Dip the loop into the flask and shake it to dislodge the yeast. Once again, flame the mouth of the flask, replace the cap, and shake the flask. Let the flask sit in a warm area for two to three days. The starter wort should turn cloudy as the yeast grows. Do not wait for the yeast to settle — that's going too far. It's now time to make a regular starter.

Micro Starter to Starter

Allow the large vessel to warm up to room temperature. Again, in your clean environment area, uncover the large vessel and pass the mouth through the flame. Repeat for the small flask. Pour the micro starter into the large vessel and attach an airlock. It should be ready for pitching in three days.

Slants

Now that you have a petri dish of a yeast colony you want to keep around, you need to put some cells onto the yeast slants for storage. This, too, must be done in the clean environment area.

Materials for Putting Cells on Yeast Slants for Storage

Petri dish with the isolated yeast colony
Four or five sterile slants (made earlier)
Inoculation loop
Flame source

Directions

1. Heat the loop to red hot.
2. Open the petri dish just wide enough to get the loop in and cool it on a sterile, unpopulated area of the petri dish.
3. With the loop, scrape up a few cells from a selected colony and then close the dish.
4. Uncap a culture tube and streak the surface of the medium with the loop.
5. Pass the mouth of the tube through the flame and recap the tube.
6. Repeat from Step 1 until you have a total of four or five tubes.
7. Seal the caps to the tubes with tape and label the tubes.

Leave the slants in a warm environment (60°–70°F) for a few days to allow the yeast to grow out. Once there is a healthy growth of yeast colonies, you can place the slants in the refrigerator for storage. They can be kept for six months before the yeast needs to be grown out again. Cover the yeast with sterile mineral oil to extend this storage time if desired. In reality, some homebrewers have stored yeast on slants for more than 12 months and have used them successfully. We think that might be pushing it a little; but if you have a good technique and a clean environment, there should be no problems with long storage. Remember: If you ever see anything other than the smooth, white or cream-colored yeast colonies growing in the tubes, discard them. There is no point in playing with contaminated items.

– Afterword –

EVOLUTION
IN ACTION

PEOPLE HAVE BEEN BREWING BEER for thousands of years. You'd think we'd have had time enough to think of every possible gadget or brewing approach imaginable, yet a look through recent homebrewing supply catalogs, brewing magazines, and other literature shows that the homebrewing gadget market is about as quiet as a three-ring circus.

As we go to press in early 1996, we see that within the short time taken to produce this book, there have been innumerable great new gadgets on the market that we only wish we could have had an opportunity to review. A couple of the most promising gadgets that have come to our attention in the last month or so include a very small refrigeration unit that's perfectly suited to a single soda keg, and a very sporty brewing stand that features a top platform that can actually be raised and lowered. The appearance of such brew ware demonstrates how very much alive the spirit of inventiveness and ingenuity is in the homebrewing community.

There are countless innovations in equipment approaches and adaptations. Some are wonderfully ingenious, and others, well, let's just say they have potential to grow to great ideas as their inventors gain experience with the hobby.

Throughout this book, we've shared our own ideas and views on various approaches. In some cases, our views reflect our own experiences and preferences, which may not match your own. Approaches that we didn't like may work well for you. Be open to trying other ideas, and maybe coming up with some new gadgets yourself. Enjoy yourself.

Cheers!

— Appendix A —

BUILDING A MOTORIZED MILL

A compact, motorized roller mill was built by Chris Barnhart of Geneseo, Illinois. This mill delivers excellent crushes that are comparable in quality to those delivered by the JSP MaltMill. Milling the grain on brew day can be as simple as turning on the mill and filling the hopper.

The authors gratefully acknowledge Chris's work on this mill and appreciate his willingness to share his plans with us. The following overview of how to build a motorized mill is used with the permission of the author (© 1995 Chris Barnhart).

OVERVIEW

The roller mill project was conceived after looking over a review of the JSP MaltMill. I figured I could probably build an adjustable mill for a lot less than the normal asking price of $130. My overall goal was to design an adjustable mill that is relatively easy to build using mostly common, easily obtained parts. As an avid woodworker and packrat I had most of the materials on hand, so my final cost was about

$57; your mileage may vary. I estimate that you can probably buy everything you need for about $100.

The mill is a two-roller design and is motor driven. One roller is powered and the other is free-spinning. Both are housed in a wooden frame. An external carriage riding in dovetail guides provides adjustability. I'll attempt to describe the mill and construction details in the text that follows.

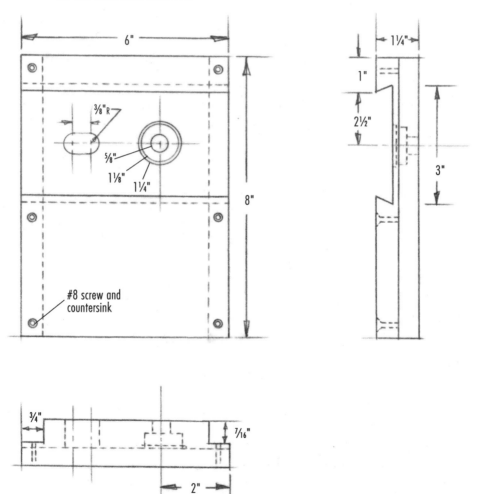

Roller mill sides (two required): The front and back panels are mirror images that fit into rabbet joints milled into the sides.

Rollers were fabricated by a local machine shop out of 2-inch diameter cold rolled steel rod for a cost of $20. Both rollers are finished with a medium diamond knurl pattern. A ½-inch border is left at each end of the rollers. Both are drilled and tapped in the center of each end to accept a ½-inch x 13 tpi (threads per inch) bolt. Rollers are supported by ½-inch diameter x 13 tpi bolts passing through ½-inch sealed ball bearings mounted in the mill frame. Spacers are required between the bearings and rollers. Spacers overcome the tendency of the bolts to overtighten into the rollers, making the mill seize. The spacers are made of ½-inch copper pipe. The pair of spacers for the free-spinning roller are ¹⁵⁄₁₆ inches long.

A short dissertation on rollers is provided. Expensive commercial mills consist of multiple pairs of rollers and screens to precisely crush malt and get an optimum ratio of grits and flour. Two-roller mills are more practical for the homebrewer. With that in mind, the design is partially dictated by the size of the roller. The larger the roller, the better the crush up to practical limits (size and weight being foremost). Large (4" to 8") rollers can be smooth or slightly rough and still be able to draw malt through the gap to crush it. Because the gap narrows gradually, the force of the rollers acts on the malt kernel at close to right angles using friction to draw it through. Small rollers don't have the gradual narrowing of the gap and must overcome the "shallower" angle by increased friction. Knurling provides the extra "bite" required to pull the malt through.

MILL

The mill frame consists of two parts: the main body and the carriage. Both are made of walnut, although any dense hardwood could be substituted. Hickory, ash, or maple would be ideal. All wooden parts of the mill are sanded and finished with water-based polyurethane. The most critical part of the mill design is ensuring the rollers are mounted level and parallel to each other in the same plane. Care must be taken when laying out and machining the bearing cups in the mill body and carriage sides. Due to the mill's design, a small amount of non-parallelism can be adjusted out with the gap-adjusting bolts.

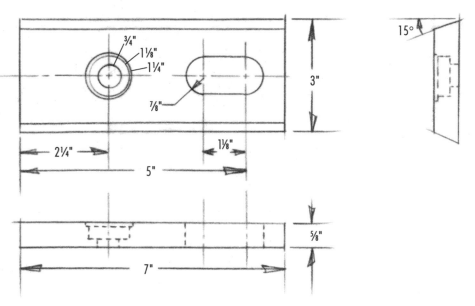

Roller mill dovetail slides (two required, left and right, mirror-image): These fit into guide slots on the main body of the mill and form part of the carriage.

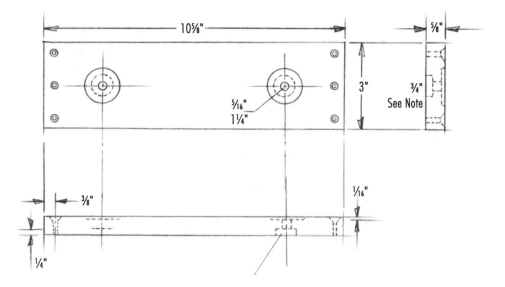

Carriage front and back panels (front shown) are secured to the dovetail slides to increase the rigidity of the mill. Note: The countersink is only required on the front panel.

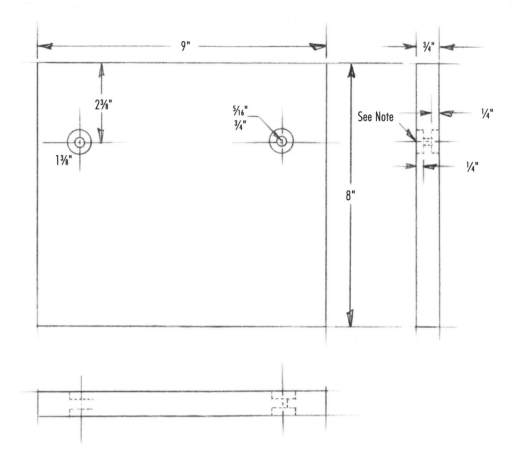

Front and back panels. *Only the front panel requires this countersink to accept tensioning spring. Note: Only front panel requires this countersink. Countersinking accepts tensioning spring.*

The main body is a rectangular box made with rabbet joints. A rabbet joint is basically a recess or shoulder cut in the edge of the board to accept another board. Rabbet joints are stronger than box joints and easier to make than dovetail joints. The front and back panels rest in the rabbet joints milled in the sides. Screws passing through the sides hold the front and back panels in place. A dovetail slot is routed in each side, parallel to the base, to hold the carriage. Bearing cups and clearance holes for the roller bolts are bored in each side.

The carriage is made with dovetail slides that fit into the guide slots on the main body of the mill. A front and back plate are secured to the dovetail slides to increase rigidity. Holes are drilled in the carriage front and back plates to hold the adjusting and lock bolts.

The exterior holes on the front and back plates are countersunk to accept fender washers. The washers reduce wear and spread the load placed on the carriage during mill operation. Bearing cups and clearance holes for the drive shaft and bolt heads are bored in the dovetail slides.

HOPPER

The hopper is fabricated from four separate pieces of masonite. It is set into a small frame of walnut that is sized to be a snug fit into the top opening of the mill body. The hopper tapers down to a 4" slot ¼" wide centered over the rollers. The hopper could alternatively be made

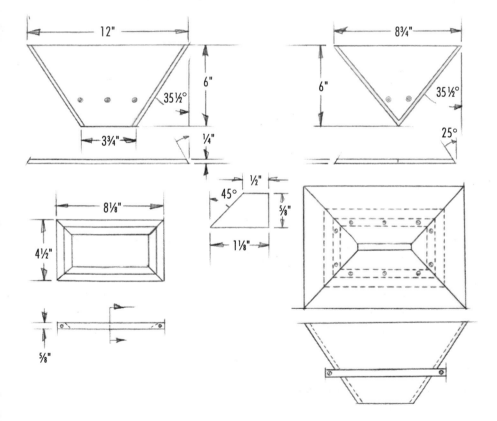

Hopper and collar. The hopper is constructed of four pieces of masonite and set into a walnut frame.

from sheet metal. A sheet metal insert is placed in the mill body between the rollers and hopper. The insert prevents stray grains from going around or behind the rollers.

BASE

The base is made from an oblong piece of particle board cut to fit over a used drywall bucket or old plastic fermenter.

A circle of slightly smaller diameter than the bucket is glued to the bottom of one end of the base and fits down into the bucket to prevent the mill from sliding around. The mill is attached to the base over a rectangular opening. The opening allows crushed grain to pass through the base into the bucket. The motor mount is also attached to the base using carriage bolts.

MOTOR

The motor is an AC gear motor with 40 inch-pounds of torque running at 177 RPM. I found this at the Surplus Center (800/488-3407). It is attached to a motor mount and then bolted to the base. The motor drives the rear roller via a belt and pulley arrangement. A 1½" pulley is used on the motor and a 2" pulley is mounted to the rear roller by passing a ½" bolt through it into the roller. I have the allen screw on the pulley tightened down on a flat land filed onto the bolt. If you are worried about rocks or debris jamming the mill, you could remove the allen screw, drill a hole through the bolt, and install a shear pin made from a copper cotter pin or rivet.

Most people I talked to recommend running a mill around 100 to 200 RPM. Faster speeds create more dust, vibration, and so on. Most motors you will encounter are either 1750 or 3450 RPM, gearmotors excepted. If you opt for a standard motor, speed reductions can be achieved using a number of pulley and v-belt combinations. I had originally planned to use a 1750 RPM motor, so the mill was designed to take up to a 10" pulley. (That's why the mill is as tall as it is.) I was going to use a 1" pulley on the motor and a 10" pulley on the drive roller for an effective speed of 175 RPM. Gearmotors have an advantage in that the speed is already reduced without elaborate pulley arrangements, a large amount of torque can be obtained from smaller motors, and the mill can be more compact. You'll want at least 30 inch-pounds of torque (or greater). The mill could alternatively be hand-cranked by attaching an appropriate handle to the ½" drive bolt.

Motor Mount

I made this from walnut as well. The type of motor you select will determine the final design. I needed a mount that would accept a face-mounted motor. The basic design can be adapted to a variety of motor sizes.

The following is a list of the tools I used: router; table saw; forstner bits (¾", ⅞", 1", 1⅛", 1¼", 1½"); countersink bit; drill press; and sander.

Materials

Walnut
Masonite
Particle board
Sandpaper
Water-based polyurethane
Wood screws (#8x2", #6x1½", #6x¾")
Bolts ½"x13 tpi: 3" (2 each), 3½" (1 each), 4" (1 each)
Carriage bolts: 2" (4 each), 2½" (2 each), 3" (2 each)
Motor mount bolts: ¼"x2" (4 each)
Lock washers: ½" (4 each) and ¼" (8 each)
Wing nuts: ¼" (4 each)
Nuts: ¼" (4 each)
Fender washers: 1" (4 each), 1¼" (4 each)
Bearings (1¼" wide x ⅜" deep): ½" (4 each)
Rollers
Motor
SPST toggle switch (Radio Shack)
Pulleys (1½" and 2")
V-belt

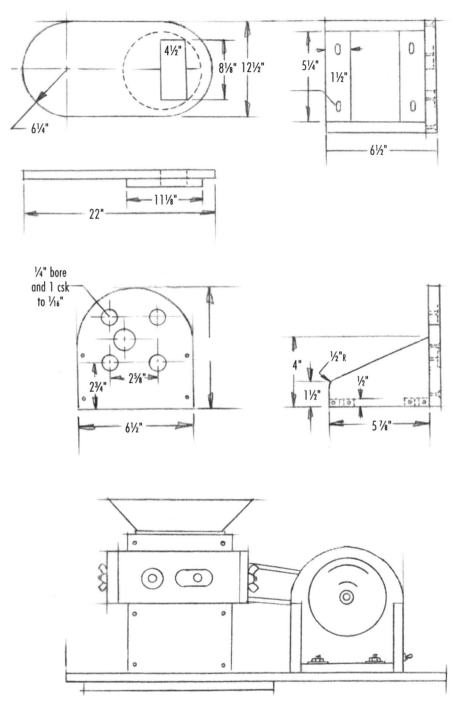

Mill and motor are mounted on a particle board base that is cut to fit over a drywall bucket.

Note on use: The gap adjustment is made by loosening the two lock bolts in the back plate of the carriage. The two bolts (gap-adjusting bolts) in the carriage front plate are turned in or out to change the gap width. An automotive feeler gauge is used to determine the correct spacing. I found that one or two passes through the mill with it set at .050 inch seemed to provide a good crush for the two-row British pale malt I use.

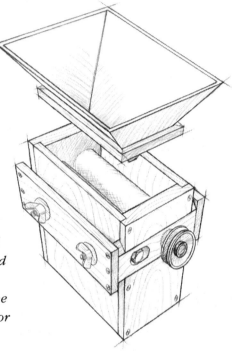

*This **motorized roller mill** has two rollers, one free and one powered, that are housed in a hardwood frame. An external carriage encloses the frame and allows the operator to make adjustments.*

— Appendix B —

METRIC CONVERSION

Use the following formulas for converting U.S. measurements to metric. Since the conversions are not exact, it's important to convert the measurements for all of the materials.

If Measurement Is	Multiply It By	To Convert To
teaspoons	4.93	milliliters
tablespoons	14.79	milliliters
fluid ounces	29.57	milliliters
cups (liquid)	236.59	milliliters
cups (liquid)	.236	liters
cups (dry)	275.31	milliliters
cups (dry)	.275	liters
quarts (liquid)	946.36	milliliters
quarts (liquid)	.946	liters
gallons	3.785	liters
ounces	28.35	grams
pounds	.454	kilograms
inches	25.4	millimeters
inches	2.54	centimeters
inches	0.0254	meters
square inch	645.16	square millimeters
square inch	6.4516	square centimeters
feet	0.3048	meters
degrees Fahrenheit	$\frac{5}{9}$(temperature − 32)	degrees Celsius (Centigrade)

While standard metric measurements for dry ingredients are given as units of mass, U.S. measurements are given as units of volume. Therefore, the conversions listed above for dry ingredients are given in the metric equivalent of volume.

— Appendix C —

SUPPLIERS

ADVANCED BREWERS SCIENTIFIC

2233 Sand Rd.
Port Clinton, OH 43452
(419) 732-2200

Sells a range of yeast culturing supplies, cultures, labware, incubator, laminar-flow hood, and more.

AMERICAN AIR FILTER

P.O. Box 35690
Louisville, KY 40232
(800) 464-8970

Sells HEPA airfilters.

AMERICAN BREWMASTER

3021-5 Stoneybrook Dr.
Raleigh, NC 27604
(919) 850-0095

General supplier; sells a digital pH meter.

BENJAMIN MACHINE PRODUCTS

338 Spenker Ave.
Modesto, CA 95354
(209) 523-8874

Sells counter-pressure bottle filler.

BEVERAGE PEOPLE

840 Pines Rd. #14
Santa Rosa, CA 95403
(707) 544-2520

Sells counter-pressure bottle filler, 3-tier all-grain brewing system, and immersion wort chillers.

BITOA BREWING SYSTEMS

Brewers Warehouse
4520 Union Bay Place N.E.
Seattle, WA 98105
(206) 527-5047

Sells cylindroconical fermenter.

BRAUKUNST

55 Lakeview Dr.
Carlton, MN 55718
(218) 384-9844 or
(800) 972-BRAU

Sells counter-pressure bottle filler, also full line of kegging accessories, tanks, and more.

Brew City Beer Gear

P.O. Box 27729
Milwaukee, WI 53227
(414) 276-5093
Sells propane burners and other supplies.

Brew Co.

P.O. Box 1063
Boone, NC 28607
Sells BruHeat boiler; manufactures and sells counterflow chiller as well as BrewCap inverted-carboy fermenter.

Brewers Resource

409 Calle San Pablo #104
Camarillo, CA 93012
(805) 445-4100 or
(800) 827-3983
Sells yeast culturing kits, slants, equipment, and more, also BrewTek malt mill. General supplier; sells aerator pump, thermostat.

Brewers Warehouse

4520 Union Bay Place N.E.
Seattle, WA 98105
(206) 527-5047
Sells turnkey brewing setup oriented around gravity-flow brewery; also complete brewery systems. Counterflow chiller ($80) and large-scale model with pump ($900).

The Brewery

11 Market St.
Potsdam, NY 13676
(800) 762-2560
Sells beer balls and tapping systems.

The Brewlab

1039 Hamilton St.
Allentown, PA 18101
(610) 821-8410 or
(800) 900-8410
Sells range of homebrew equipment; owner has used oak barrels to age homebrew.

Chateau Distributors

P.O. Box 2683
Sumas, WA 98295 or,
P.O. Box 8000-391
Abottsford, BC V2S 6H1
(604) 882-9692
Manufactures bottle washers.

Cumberland General Store

Route 3
Crossville, TN 38555
(615) 484-8481 or
(800) 334-4640
Sells copper kettles, wooden barrels, and bungs.

Davison Manufacturing

4025 S. 65th #14
Greenfield, WI 53220
(414) 545-9246
Makes color slides for beer color evaluation.

East Coast Brewing Supply

P.O. Box 060904
Staten Island, NY 10306
(718) 667-4459
Sells complete brewing systems, also brew kettles and burners.

FERMENTAP

P.O. Box 30175
Stockton, CA 95213
(209) 942-2750

Manufactures and sells inverted-carboy fermenter.

FERMENTHAUS

P.O. Box 4220
Victoria, BC V8X 3X8
(604) 386-1023

Manufactures bottle washers.

FERMTECH

2 Stewart St. #7
Kitchener, Ontario N2G2E4
(519) 570-2163

Manufactures Double-Blast bottle washer and other gizmos.

THE FILTER STORE PLUS

P.O. Box 425
Rush, NY 14543
(800) 828-1494

Sells a wide range of filters.

FOXX EQUIPMENT

421 Southwest Blvd.
Kansas City, MO 64108
(816) 421-3600

Sells beverage tapping equipment including counter-pressure bottle filler; manufactures and sells a complete line of kegging equipment including all gaskets, lines, and fittings.

FRESHOPS

36180 Kings Valley Hwy.
Philomath, OR 97370
(541) 929-2736
FAX (541) 929-2702

Sells hops rhizomes.

GRAINGER

333 Knightsbridge Pkwy.
Lincolnshire, IL 60069
(800) 225-5994

Sells a wide range of motors, pipes, fittings, pumps, and more.

HEART'S HOME BEER & WINE MAKING SUPPLY

5824 North Orange Blossom Trail
Orlando, FL 32810
(407) 298-4103

Sells counterflow chiller ($70), complete keg systems, and other equipment.

THE HOME BREWERY

P.O. Box 730
Ozark, MO 65721
(800) 321-BREW

Sells immersion chiller ($30).

JACK SCHMIDLING PRODUCTIONS

18016 Church Rd.
Marengo, IL 60152
(815) 923-0031

Manufactures JSP MaltMill roller mill and EasyMasher.

JET CARBOY & BOTTLE WASHER CO.

3301 Veterans Dr.
Traverse City, MI 49684
(616) 935-4555

Sells brass pressure bottle washer.

JOHNSON CONTROLS

507 East Michigan St.
P.O. Box 423
Milwaukee, WI 53201
(414) 228-1200

Sells thermostats.

KOCH'S KONCEPTS

Larry Koch
9510 Bruce Drive
Silver Spring, MD 20901
(301) 587-5293
Sells RIMS setup.

LEHMAN'S HARDWARE

P.O. Box 41
Kidron, OH 44636
(216) 857-5757
Sells wooden barrels, bungs, and spigots.

LISTERMANN MANUFACTURING

1621 Dana Ave.
Cincinnati, OH 45212
(513) 731-1130
Manufactures PhilMill roller mill; Phil's Phalse Bottom, Phil's Philler, Phil's Lauter Tun, Sparger, and Phil's Psyphon Starter.

MARCON FILTERS

120 Woodstream Blvd., Unit 1
Woodbridge, Ontario L4L 7Z1
(905) 264-1494
Sells pressurized plate filter systems; also sells a magnetic pump.

McMASTER CARR

P.O. Box 440
New Brunswick, NJ 08903
(908) 329-3200
Sells a wide range of hose fittings, quick disconnects, pumps, fittings, and more.

NORTH HARBOR MANUFACTURING

53 North Harbor Rd.
Colchester, VT 05446
(802) 893-7500
Sells beer chiller (jockey box).

PICO-BREWING SYSTEMS

8383 Geddes Rd.
Ypsilanti, MI 48198
(313) 482-8565
FAX (313) 485-2739
Sells complete brewing setups including tiered stands; also complete brewing setups and modified beer kegs, modified kegs for fermenters.

QUOIN INDUSTRIAL

401 Violet St.
Golden, CO 80401
(303) 279-8731
Manufactures Party Pig.

RAPIDS WHOLESALE EQUIPMENT

P.O. Box 396
Cedar Rapids, IA 52406
(800) 553-7906
Sells homebrewing equipment kit, CO_2 regulators, CO_2 canisters, gas burners, and an assortment of kettles.

SABCO INDUSTRIES

4511 South Ave.
Toledo, OH 43615
(419) 531-5347
FAX (419) 531-7765
sabco@kegs.com
http://www.kegs.com
Sells used kegs, a turnkey RIMS system, and kegs modified for use as homebrewing vessels.

Stein Fillers LLC

4180 Viking Way
Long Beach, CA 90808
(310) 425-0588

Superb Gas Products

48 Empire Dr.
Belleville, IL 62220
(800) 233-0255

Sells gas burners and accessories.

Surplus Center

1015 West O St.
P.O. Box 82209
Lincoln, NE 68501-2209
(800) 488-3407

Sells motors and an ever-changing assortment of equipment.

Tkach Enterprises

P.O. Box 344
Castle Rock, CO 80104
(303) 660-2297

Manufactures adhesive liquid crystal "Fermometer" temperature strips.

United States Plastics

1390 Neubrecht Road
Lima, OH 45801
(800) 537-9724

Sells cylindroconical plastic vessels, tubes, Gatt coolers, and other plastic devices.

Valley Brewing Equipment

1310 Surrey Ave.
Ottawa, Ontario K1V6S9
(613) 733-5241

Manufactures Valley Roller Mill.

Vinotheque

2142 Trans Canada Highway
Dorval, Quebec H9P2N4
(514) 684-1331

Sells a range of equipment, including fermenters, carboys, caps, and bottle fillers.

West Creek Home Brewing

118 Washington Ave.
P.O. Box 623
Endicott, NY 13761-0623
(607) 785-4233

Sells CO_2 tap for PET bottle and Tap-A-Keg.

Williams Brewing

P.O. Box 2195
San Leandro, CA 94577
(800) 759-6025

Sells range of equipment and supplies.

Wine Enthusiast

8 Sawmill River Road
Hawthorne, NY 10532
(800) 356-8466

Sells wine cellars that can be used as fermentation rooms.

Yeast Culture Kit Company

1308 W. Madison
Ann Arbor, MI 48103
(313) 761-5914

Sells range of yeast culturing supplies.

GLOSSARY

Adjunct: Any grain other than malted barley used as a starch source or for flavoring properties.

Airlock: Device that fits into a vessel's lid and that is filled with water or other liquids, enabling expanding gas inside a fermenter to escape without allowing outside air into the vessel.

Aerate: To dissolve air in a liquid.

Alpha Acid: Resin from hops that provides bitterness in beer.

Aluminum: Lightweight metal sometimes used for brew kettles or other vessels.

Autoclave: A pressurized, steam-heated vessel or chamber used for sterilization of equipment or material.

Boiling: The step in brewing at which the dilute solution of sugars and water is concentrated and hops are added.

Brewing: Craft and science of making beer.

Bright Beer Tanks: Storage tanks for clear, finished beer.

Carbon Filter: Filter used to remove chlorine from water.

Carbonate: To inject or dissolve carbon dioxide gas into beer.

Carboy: A large glass bottle (usually 5 or more gallons) in which beer can be fermented.

Caustic: Corrosive chemical.

Channeling: Tendency of liquid draining through a grain bed to carve a single path and then follow it without permeating the grain bed.

Chiller: Piece of equipment that cools hot wort rapidly before pitching yeast. See also Heat Exchanger.

Chlorine: Element used in dilute form as a sanitizing agent. Commonly present in municipal water sources, where it is used to kill bacteria.

Closed Fermentation: Fermentation process conducted in a sealed vessel with airlocks or other pressure-relief devices.

Conditioning: Process of carbonating a beer.

Conversion: The saccharification, or breakdown, of starches to fermentable sugars.

Copper: Material traditionally used in brewing equipment fabrication. Also a necessary yeast nutrient, but one that can kill yeast at excessive levels.

Counterflow: Method of heat exchange by which two liquids of different temperatures flow in opposite directions along a path separated by conductive material.

Crush: Process of milling grain. The quality (granularity and husk integrity) of milled grain.

Cylindroconical: Describes the shape of fermenters in most commercial breweries; a cylinder capped at one end by a cone.

Decoction: Mashing method that involves removing part of the mash, boiling it, and returning it to the main mashing vessel.

Degree of Extract: Measure of mash yield or efficiency: the specific gravity of one gallon of wort made from one pound of malt.

Diatomaceous Earth: Sandy, silicate substance made up of skeletons of minute colonies of algae, called "diatoms." Used as a filtering medium and available in different grades.

Distillation: Purification of liquid by boiling and condensing. When used to purify brewing water, will remove all ions.

Endosperm: Starchy center matter of a barleycorn.

Enzyme: Complex protein that acts as a catalyst to break starches, sugars, or other complex molecules into simpler components.

Extract: Sugars derived from grain in a mashing process. Commonly used to refer to a commercially prepared syrup or powder of such sugars.

Fermentation: Process in which yeast obtains energy in the absence of oxygen by breaking down sugar into carbon dioxide and alcohol.

Fermenter: Vessel or tank in which the fermentation process takes place.

Filter: Porous membrane or layer through which liquid is pumped, removing impurities or sediment.

Finings: Additives used to clarify a beer.

Glycol: An anti-freeze used in fermenter jackets and some heat exchangers.

Grist: The crushed malts and adjuncts that are mixed with hot water to form the mash.

Heat Exchanger: Piece of brewing equipment used to heat or cool the wort or beer.

Hopback: A chamber in the middle of the siphon line that contains fresh hops and through which the brewer runs the hot wort.

Hops: The flowers (or cones) of the female hop plant, used in brewing to impart bitter flavors to the beer, balancing the sweet malt.

Hot Break: Flocculation of protein and other matter during the boil.

Hydrometer: Measuring device used to determine the amount of dissolved sugar and other solid matter in a solution.

Infusion: Mashing method in which grain is mixed with hot water.

Iodophor: A dilute solution of iodine and phosphoric acid used as a sanitizing agent.

Ion: An atom or bound group of atoms that carries an electrical charge.

Iron: Ion that causes haze and hampers yeast.

Isomerize: To alter the arrangement, but not the kind or number, of atoms in a compound by heating or other means. In brewing, hop alpha acids are isomerized in the boil.

Jockey Box: Cooler with beer taps attached to the outside. Beer runs through cooling tubes or a cold plate inside the cooler.

Keg: Vessel used for storing and dispensing finished beer. Homebrewers typically use small soda kegs of about 5 gallons. U.S. commercial breweries typically use half-barrel kegs of 15.5 gallons. Common keg sizes will vary in other countries.

Kettle: Large vessel, usually made of stainless steel or copper, in which the wort is boiled.

Kiln: Large furnace with a perforated floor heated by either fire or heaters, in which malt is dried and roasted.

Knurl: Cut edges, grooves, or patterns used to roughen a smooth surface, thereby providing friction.

Kraeusen: (1) The large head of foam that forms on the surface of the wort during the early stages of fermentation. (2) Method of carbonation in which unfermented beer is added to finished beer to bring about a second fermentation.

Lager: To age beer at low temperatures for a period of weeks or months.

Lauter Tun: Large vessel with perforated false bottom used to strain the sweet liquid from grain after mashing.

Lead: Toxic metal occasionally found in some alloys and sometimes present as an ion in water.

Malt: Barley or other grain that is allowed to germinate, developing enzymes and sugars needed for brewing.

Malting: Process of soaking, sprouting, drying, and roasting barley to render it suitable for brewing.

Mash: The process of mixing crushed grains with hot water to convert starch to sugar. Also, the mixture of water and grain.

Mill: (1) Device used to crush grain. (2) Process of crushing whole grains. Process of crushing whole grains

Open Fermentation: Fermentation process conducted in a non-sealed vessel, often in shallow vats, open to the air.

Oxidation: Any chemical reaction in which oxygen reacts with another substance.

pH: Potential hydrogen. A measure of alkalinity or acidity where 7 is neutral, lower numbers are acid, and higher numbers are alkaline.

Pitch: To add yeast to a cooled wort.

Priming: To add sugar to finished beer, inducing a second fermentation and producing carbon dioxide.

PVC: Plastic (polyvinyl chloride) used by homebrewers in hoses, such as siphons and beverage lines, and in plumbing pipes.

Rack: To transfer wort or beer from one container to another, separating clear liquid from sediment.

Recirculation: Action of pumping wort from the bottom of the mash tun to the surface. Used to clarify the wort. Also called "vorlauf."

Saccharification: The conversion of starches to sugars by enzyme action.

Sanitary: Clean and nearly free of microbes; reducing risk of infection.

Single Infusion: Mashing process that involves holding the mash at one temperature step (about 148 to 154°F) until starches convert to sugars.

Siphon: Moving liquid from one vessel to another by means of gravity and a vacuum.

Slant: See Yeast Slant.

Sparging: Rinsing spent grains with hot water to recover as much sugar as possible. The process of obtaining clear wort from mash, including runoff, recirculation, and rinsing.

Specific Gravity: The density of wort: a measurement of the amount of sugars in solution.

Starter: A small volume of wort to which yeast is added, increasing its quantity before pitching.

Steeping: Soaking barley or other grains in water.

Step Mash: Mashing method that involves two or more temperature rests, beginning with the lower temperature, and increasing by means of direct heat or infusion of hotter water.

Sterile: Totally devoid of life. More exacting standard than "sanitary."

Strike Heat: Temperature of mash water before mixing with grain. Water at the appropriate temperature is called "strike water."

Tin: Metal often found in solders; can cause haze.

Trub: Sediment.

Underletting: Filling the area below a false bottom in a lauter tun with hot water before adding the mash.

Vinyl: Plastic (polyvinyl chloride) used by homebrewers for siphon hoses, beverage lines, and other purposes.

Whirlpool: Tank into which beer is pumped at pressure, causing a spinning motion that settles out trub.

Wort: The solution of malt sugars, water, and other compounds produced by the mashing process.

Yeast: Single cell fungus capable of fermentation.

Yeast Slant: Test tube, dish, or similar container of gelatin and growth medium (wort), prepared under sterile conditions, in which pure yeast strains are grown and stored.

Yield: Percentage by weight of the malt that will be converted to soluble substances (sugars) in the mash kettle.

FURTHER READING

MAGAZINES AND ARTICLES

Brew Your Own. P.O. Box 1504, Martinez, CA 94553–9932. Fax 510-372-8582.

Brewing Techniques. Box 322, Eugene, OR 97403. 1-800-427-2993.

Busch, Jim. "Fundamentals of Home Brewery Design." *Brewing Techniques,* January/February 1995, Vol. 3, No. 1, page 20.

———. "Open Fermentation Alternatives." *Zymurgy,* Fall 1994, Vol. 17, No. 3, page 44.

Caldwell, Jim. "How to Build a Laminar Flow Hood for as Little as $100." *Brewing Techniques,* May/June 1995, page 18.

Cantwell, Dick, Fal Allen, and Kevin Forhan. "Beer from the Stainless." *Brewing Techniques,* November/December 1993, Vol. 1, No. 4, page 22.

Caplan, Bob. "A Three-Tiered Gravity-Flow Brewing System." *Brewing Techniques,* March/April 1994, Vol. 2, No. 2, page 44.

Daniels, Steve. "How to Build a Simple Counter Pressure Bottle Filler." *Zymurgy,* Spring 1990, Vol. 13, No. 1, page 36.

Dawson, Bennet. "Closed System Home Brewing." *Brewing Techniques,* July/August 1994, Vol. 2, No. 4, page 48.

Denke, Kurt. "Taming the Wild Fridge." *Zymurgy,* Fall 1989, Vol. 12, No. 3, page 36.

Donaghue, Jeff. "Testing Your Metal — Is Aluminum Hazardous to Your Beer?" *Brewing Techniques,* January/February 1995, Vol. 3, No. 1, page 62.

Fahrendorf, Teri. "Closed System Pressurized Fermentation." *Zymurgy,* Special Issue 1994, Vol. 15, No. 4, page 64.

———. "The Jockeybox." *Zymurgy,* Special Issue 1992, Vol. 15, No. 4.

Farnsworth, Paul. "Yeast Stock Maintenance and Starter Culture Production." *Zymurgy,* Special Issue 1989, page 32.

Fleming, Phil. "Immersion Style Wort Chiller." *Zymurgy,* Special Issue 1992, Vol. 15, No. 4, page 60.

Goeres, Mindy, and Ross Goeres. "Wort Chillers: Three Styles to Improve Your Brew." *Zymurgy,* Spring 1992, Vol. 15, No. 1, page 38.

Gorman, Bob, Steve Stroud, and Mike Fertsch. "Roll Out the Mills." *Zymurgy,* Fall 1994, Vol. 17, No. 3, page 32.

Hauptli, Kerry. "What about RIMS." *Zymurgy,* Special Issue 1995, Vol. 18, No. 4.

Humbert, Richard. "The Wort Rocker: A Simple Device for Wort Aeration." *Brewing Techniques,* March/April 1995, page 17.

Johnson, Sam. "An Easy-to-Build Mashing System for Precise Temperature Control." *Brewing Techniques,* July/August 1995, Vol. 3, No. 4, page 16.

Liddil, Jim, and John Palmer. "A Complete Guide to Cleaning and Sanitation." *Zymurgy,* Fall 1995, Vol. 18, No. 3, page 38.

Manning, Martin. "Modifying Half Barrel Kegs for Use as Brewing Vessels." *Brewing Techniques,* March/April 1994, Vol. 2, No. 2, page 40.

Martin, Cy. "Racking from Carboys to Soda Kegs." *Zymurgy,* Winter 1989, Vol. 12, No. 5, page 26.

Miller, Dave. "Ask the Troubleshooter: Jockey Boxes at Home." *Brewing Techniques,* January/February 1995, Vol. 3, No. 1, page 29.

———. "Ask the Troubleshooter: Keg Carbonation." *Brewing Techniques,* January/February 1994, Vol. 2, No. 1, page 14.

Millspaw, Micah. "The Care and Feeding of Stainless Steel." *Brewing Techniques,* July/August 1994, Vol. 2, No. 4, page 44.

Morris, Rodney. "Recirculating Infusion Mash System Revisited." *Zymurgy,* Special Issue 1992, Vol. 15, No. 4, page 49.

Mosher, Randy. "Working with Brewery Materials." *Zymurgy,* Special Issue 1992, Vol. 15, No. 4, page 7.

O'Conner, Kieran. "The In-Laws Refrigerator." *Brewing Techniques,* November/December 1993, page 45.

O'Neil, Dave. "Beer Tree: A Three-Tiered System with Roots in Simplicity." *Brewing Techniques,* March/April 1994, Vol. 2, No. 2, page 47.

Palmer, John, and Paul Prozinski. "Fluid Dynamics — A Simple Key to Mastery of Efficient Lautering." *Brewing Techniques,* July/August 1995, Vol. 3, No. 4, page 66.

Rager, Jackie. "Soda Keg Draft Systems: Better Than Bottles?" *Zymurgy,* Winter 1989, Vol. 12, No. 5, page 24.

Ruggiero, David, Jonathan Spillane, and Doug Snyder. "The Counterpressure Connection." *Zymurgy,* Fall 1995, Vol. 18, No. 3, page 56.

Schmidling, Jack. "Mashing Made Easy." *Brewing Techniques,* May/June 1994, Vol. 2, No. 3, page 46.

Smith, Quentin. "Sanitation." *Zymurgy,* Fall 1991, Vol. 14, No. 3, page 28.

Stackhouse, Charlie. "Aroma Hop Back." *Zymurgy,* Fall 1994, Vol. 17, No. 3, page 30.

Westemeier, Ed. "A Bottler's Guide to Kegging." *Zymurgy,* Summer 1995, Vol. 18, No. 2, page 46.

Zymurgy. American Homebrewers Association, P.O. Box 1679, Boulder, CO 80302–1679, (303) 447-0816.

Books about Beer and Brewing

Beaumont, Stephen. *A Taste for Beer.* Pownal, VT: Storey Publishing, 1995.

deClerck, Jean. *A Textbook of Brewing.* London: Chapman & Hall, 1957.

Eames, Alan D. *Secret Life of Beer: Legends, Lore & Little-Known Facts*. Pownal, VT: Storey Publishing, 1995.

Fisher, Joe, and Dennis Fisher. *Great Beer from Kits*. Pownal, VT: Storey Publishing, 1996.

Foster, Terry. *Pale Ale*. Boulder, CO: Brewers Publications, 1989.

Garetz, Mark. *Using Hops*. Danville, CA: HopTech, 1994.

Lutzen, Karl F., and Mark Stevens. *Homebrew Favorites: A Coast-to-Coast Collection of more than 240 Beer and Ale Recipes*. Pownal, VT: Storey Publishing, 1994.

Miller, Dave. *Brewing the World's Great Beers: A Step-by-Step Guide*. Pownal, VT: Storey Publishing, 1992.

———. *The Complete Handbook of Home Brewing*. Pownal, VT: Storey Publishing, 1988.

———. *Dave Miller's Homebrewing Guide*. Pownal, VT: Storey Publishing, 1995.

———. "Setting Up Your Home Kegging System," in *Just Brew It! Beer and Brewing*, 1992, Vol. 12. Boulder, CO: Brewers Publications.

Mosher, Randy. *The Brewer's Companion*. Seattle, WA: Alephanalia Publications, 1993.

Nachel, Marty. *Beer Across America: A Regional Guide to Brewpubs and Microbreweries*. Pownal, VT: Storey Publishing, 1995.

Noonan, Greg. *Brewing Lager Beer*. Boulder, CO: Brewers Publications, 1986.

Owens, Bill. *How to Build a Small Brewery: Draft Beer in Ten Days*. Hayward, CA: Bill Owens, 1982, 1992.

Papazian, Charlie. *The Homebrewer's Companion*. New York: Avon Books, 1994.

———. *The New Complete Joy of Homebrewing*. New York: Avon Books, 1991.

Reese, M. R. *Better Beer and How to Brew It*. Pownal, VT: Garden Way Publishing, 1978.

Smith, Gregg. *The Beer Enthusiast's Guide: Tasting & Judging Brews from Around the World*. Pownal, VT: Storey Publishing, 1994.

Index

Italic page numbers = Illustrations

Glass
  fermenters, 19, 140
  pros and cons of, 19
  thermometers, 35, *35*
Glatt Mill, 55–56, *55*
Glove box, 220–21, *221*
Gott cooler, 70, 71
Grains, storing, 45
Grolsch swing-top bottles, 159
Grommets, 139
Ground fault circuit interrupt
    (GFCI), 24, 79
Growlers, 181, *181*

H

Heat exchanger, 11
Heat shroud, 93–94, *94*
High Efficiency Particulate Air
    (HEPA) filters, 221–22, *222*
High-gravity brewing method, 11
Hole driller, directions for making,
    127–28, *127*
Hop(s)
  adding, 3
  drying, 204–9, *209*
  storing, 45
  trellises and poles for, 201–4,
    202, 203
  utilization, 36
Hopbacks, 97–99, *99*
Hopper construction, 61–63, *62,
    234–35, *234*
Hose counterflow chiller, 117–19,
    119
Hoses
  aeration, 150–51, *151*
  connecting, 13–14, *13*
Hunter Airstat, 134, 136
Hunter Energy Monitor, 134
Hydrometers, 7, *8*
  density measurement and,
    36–38, *37, 38*

I

Ice, adding directly to wort, 103–4
Immersion chillers. *See* Chillers,
    immersion
Inoculation loop, 215–16, *216,
    224, *224*
Iodine test, 39
Iodophor, 14, 15–16, 20, 166, 186
Isomerization, 3, 86

J

Jet washer, 163, *163*
Jockey boxes, 111, 193–95, *195*
JSP EasyMasher, 71, 76–77, *77, 84,
    140
JSP EasySparger, 83–84, *84*
JSP MaltMill, 51, 53–54, *53*

K

Kegging
  advantages over bottling, 182
  cost and components of a
    system, 182–85, *183*
Kegs
  ball-valve, 190–91
  bungs, removing, 190
  bungs, replacing, 191–92, *192*
  Carbonator, 188–89, *189*
  connectors, 185
  Cornelius, 153–54, 184
  5-liter mini-, 179–80, *179*
  jockey boxes, 111, 193–95, *195*
  modifying refrigerators for,
    197–99, *199*
  pin and ball locks on, 184, *184*
  quarter-barrel, 189–90
  refurbishing used, 187–88
  sanitizing, 185–86
  sizes of, 184
  sources for, 184–85
  stainless-steel, 154, 183